Living Lines

Living Lines

Reflections by Missy Carter

Design by Joseph Moore
Typeset in Adobe Minion
Printed by the Espresso Book Machine
at The Harvard Book Store

Cover painting by Missy Carter
Back cover photograph by
Anja Langbein-Park

ISBN: 978-0-692-00980-2

Note about the Cover
One day several years ago, I was painting a
butterfly in the studio of Kitty Pechet, when
she said to me, "Missy, you are a subtle person
and I know there is boldness within you. Your
butterfly is an opportunity to display that
boldness." Her observation encouraged me
to introduce the color red to my canvas. So it
is with this collection of Living Lines, I have
determined to emerge from my subtle self
and be bold in sharing my reflections on life
and living. The butterfly is my symbol.

Thanks to my family and friends
who form the loving circle of my life,
especially to Marsh for being at the center.

Thanks to Annette LaMond, my editorial collaborator, who brought joy to the process and added richness to *Living Lines,* helping it grow from a monologue to a dialogue.

Thanks to Joe Moore, graphic designer, who brought together the elements of my butterfly painting and the words of *Living Lines* (and the space around them) into a whole reflecting the spirit in which I began this project.

Contents

The Long Way Around

These reflections were written or collected over a period of 10 years. Many are my own writings; some, written by others, expressed my feelings at the time that I read them, and still do. In the beginning, I had no idea of showing these personal reflections to others or even of saving them. But save them I did, tucking pieces of paper into files or notebooks. Occasionally, I would reread one or two, more if I had time. I found that they allowed me to revisit earlier times in my life, with the perspective of added experience. About five years ago, I began to archive my papers and to think of these reflections as "life" lines, then "living" lines. As I organized, I felt the desire to share my "living" lines with friends. Friends, in turn, encouraged me to organize them into a book, and the name came to be capitalized in my thoughts. Thus, my title—Living Lines.

Reflections collected, I realized that I needed to introduce myself. As is true of others, who have called many places home, my friends know me in various ways. So here I reintroduce myself to friends at the same time that I offer an introduction for others who don't know me. It is my hope that these words about my background will make the reflections that follow more meaningful to readers.

Writing about oneself is difficult, no matter one's age. Last year, I took a course entitled "Writing Your Spiritual Autobiography." Although the course did not lead me to recover lost or repressed memories, the weeks of focused reflection made me see parallels between events in my life. I also saw more clearly how my perception of God has evolved and my spiritual life has developed. The course renewed my determination to share my story and put Living Lines into a format that might be helpful to others.

For me, each thought or meditation is at its core spiritual. Over time, I have come to view my life as both a spiritual and religious journey. In the process of writing my spiritual autobiography, I found that I was also tracing my growth from traditional Catholicism, which—like any organized religion—can sometimes be more about fear than love, to

1

finding my own spirituality. Over the years, my own approach to religion has become more personal and ecumenical. Opening myself to others' spiritual practices and reexamining my own Catholicism, I have come to think of myself as a Catholic ecumenist.

My life's journey has been an internal trip, and also externally, a very peripatetic one. There have been psychological complexities, physical adventures and emotional challenges. I was a first child, a World War II baby. My parents had met as graduate students— my mother was studying for a master's degree in social work and my father was a medical student —and married after a four-year courtship. Whatever wishes and expectations they had for married life, war intervened. When I was just five and a half months, we started a gypsy-like moving around to military bases around the country—sixteen in all—where my father, who was an Army doctor, was dispatched to take care of troops. Our moves continued until I was nearly four years old.

I have no real memories of those early years, only images from photographs with addresses on the back. Two stories were regularly recounted and made a lasting impression. At one post, my father came down with pneumonia and was hospitalized just as his unit was shipped overseas. These men were headed for a landing at Normandy two weeks after D-Day. His unit fought at the Battle of the Bulge in December 1944—the bloodiest battle experienced by U.S. forces in the war—and not one of them returned. Though we continued our nomadic existence, my father never went overseas. After the war came the years when he was busy establishing his civilian medical practice shuttling between two hospitals, one in New York City and one in Westchester County where we lived. Meanwhile, our family expanded; by my 10th birthday, I had two sisters and a brother.

Another story that captured my imagination—often told by my mother—was of driving across the desert in a sandstorm. Mindful now of the saying, "Once you start crossing the desert, you cannot go back," I think of those millions of grains of sand pelting the car as we made that drive. That image helps me whenever I ask God for the grace to stay on my spiritual journey, reminding me that sometimes I cannot see through my own front window.

A disciplined childhood was a prelude to, and preparation for, my later role as a military officer's wife during my early adult years. From the outside, I appeared to be the model child with a model family. Yet, I lived in fear much of the time. As the oldest, I took on the responsibility of trying to help manage the household, one that was run to very high standards of orderliness. We children were expected to work very hard in school, to behave with self-restraint, and to respect my father's need for quiet and rest, after his long days with patients. At Catholic school—Immaculate Conception and then the Ursuline School, I tried to follow the rules, my goal to be perfect as my Heavenly Father was Perfect—the only way we were taught to get to heaven. Any deviation from perfection, as I perceived it, gave me more internal turmoil. I tried very hard to be good in everything, more out of the fear of God than as an expression of His love.

At home, the message was that life was hard, even painful. Because my father was a doctor, I was aware of how much pain and suffering his patients endured, so there was no room to feel sorry for myself. Of course, I have many happy memories of my childhood. And I realize now that my parents' love of classical music and art, and their enjoyment of beauty softened the regimentation of our intense home life. Still, as I reached adolescence, I knew that I didn't want to live my whole life suppressing my feelings. I daydreamed about ways I might have a career, travel and have fun.

When I went to college in 1960, I could not have imagined the social upheavals that would unfold over the next decade. I went to a college not too far from home, Manhattanville, sheltered even by the standards of the time. Early in my sophomore year, a late night phone call offered the possibility of a blind date at West Point. That sounded like fun and I said, yes. Although my date, who was in his senior year, and I had a nice weekend, he did not call or write afterward. When several of his friends asked him for my address, he thought that maybe he should have another look. That second date started a courtship that was very stormy. Marsh, the son and grandson of Army generals, didn't think I was suited to a military life and he knew how important my faith was to me (he wasn't Catholic), so he broke up with me a dozen times, sometimes sending me flowers with a card saying "Let's part friends."

After a long period of not seeing each other, Marsh called and asked if we could get together and talk. That was November of my junior year, and on New Year's Eve, we became engaged. During the spring of my senior year with plans to marry Marsh after graduation, I had to have surgery. It was not a moment when I wanted to be slowed by a hospital stay and quiet recovery. But the parallels of two life-changing events were the first of a pattern of sad and happy milestones occurring twin-like and challenging me to learn to trust God.

Marsh and I were married just before I turned 22. (Marsh was two and a half years older, and a Marine Corps second lieutenant.) We began our life together in a small, attached apartment near Camp Lejeune in North Carolina, a state that was roiling with racial tension. During the first seven years of our marriage, my husband was overseas more than 48 months, with two 13-month tours in Vietnam. On the first of those tours, he was wounded. Miraculously, the land mine that he stepped on malfunctioned and his wounds were not severe. Many friends were not so fortunate, and the losses of husbands and fathers were all too frequent. Out of the 20 lieutenants whose families were neighbors, only three returned to their families. Mourning their losses clouded many days, and nights could bring dreams in which the green cars associated with the news of death stopped at my house. During those years, we experienced the joy of welcoming our two children into the world, but an introduction to parental anxiety, too, as both infants suffered critical illnesses.

Looking back, I feel strongly that my faith in God held me together. Still, I wondered how my desire for a freer life from the one I knew as a child had become so full of events that put not just me, but also my husband, our children, and so many friends, on the precipice. One memory of this time is symbolic. Just after the birth of my daughter, a nun gave her to me to hold for the first time and asked for permission to baptize her. Stunned, but calm, my husband and I recited the "Our Father" together. Now, each time I say the prayer and come to the line, "Thy will be done," I think of that moment when those words were the hardest ones that I ever said—my heart full of hopes and fears for my baby—while I tried to trust God.

When my husband was in Vietnam the first time, my infant daughter and I lived at Marine Corps Base Camp Pendelton in Southern California, where I formed a women's group of neighbors and other women whom I had met at the Overseas Wives Club. We thought of ourselves as "old consciences and new intellects." The Second Ecumenical Council of the Vatican, known as Vatican II, convened by Pope John XXXIII in 1962, and closed by Pope Paul VI in 1965, had changed some of the rigidity of the Church. Yet, many of us were struggling with teachings concerning birth control and other life concerns. I remembered that group recently when a Jesuit friend remarked—facetiously, but tellingly—that, from the fourth century, Catholics were told that we were all going to hell until Vatican II refocused us on God's love and forgiveness as the most important tenets of the Church. It was a difficult transition—one that still holds my attention and affects my relationship with God.

Living Lines

Between my husband's two Vietnam tours, more changes came to us. Marsh went to graduate school, which had its own intense demands on the two of us. Our second child—a son—was born, and our daughter became an older sister. And my husband converted to Catholicism. When he returned to Vietnam at the end of this interlude, the children, ages four and one-and-a-half, and I moved to New York to live with my parents. Returning to my childhood home brought familiar comforts and support to me as a young "single" mother, but at the same time, I missed my husband and the intense friendships of the military bases that had been home for five years.

While my husband and I were immersed in that horrible war, other people thought they knew Vietnam through the nightly television broadcasts that entered their livings rooms each night. For many people, the cataclysms of the sixties—the assassination of President Kennedy, the civil rights movement, women's liberation, anti-war demonstrations, and more assassinations—define their memories of the time. For me, reality was altered. Although I certainly paid attention to the upheavals in the larger world, my daily life was focused on the immediate concerns of trying to make my children's lives as normal as possible and being a support to my husband. Central was my trust that God would take care of our family.

When my husband returned from Vietnam in 1971, we bought our first house and tried to adopt the rhythms of a normal suburban life. Up to that time, our lives had been anything but normal. Indeed, my husband was often very withdrawn. Post-traumatic stress disorder had not been defined or acknowledged. Nor was there support for families who had lived with the real impact of Vietnam. So we struggled to bring normalcy to our lives, fixing up our home, being with our children, making friends—all without the benefit of counseling that is more accepted and available now.

Although my faith sustained me, I was also seeking ways to grow spiritually. It was a time when folk-music Masses were new and we were young and excited by the possibilities. We joined with nine other families, celebrating Mass in our homes and teaching our children their CCD lessons. [CCD stands for Confraternity of Catholic Doctrine.] All of us had been raised in churches where Mass was celebrated by a priest who recited the liturgy in Latin and stood apart at an altar, with back turned to the congregation. We embraced our participatory liturgy. For us, this new kind of ritual was full of meaning. The children made the communion bread and wrote the songs. And a young priest came to our homes. During this time, I also took my first post-college job as a director of casework with an emergency pregnancy counseling service.

Disillusioned with the leadership in the military after the Vietnam War, my husband applied for a White House Fellowship in hopes of sharing the lessons he had learned with policymakers. Not one to be discouraged, he applied four years in a row before being selected in 1975. Marsh spent the year working for the Agency for International Development, responding to disasters and going on special assignments to Saharan Africa, Israel and Egypt. As a spouse with two young children, I experienced a whirlwind year, too. The spouses (wives and one husband) had their own program, which I helped coordinate. My days were often full of lectures and visits to government departments. One regret. Although my mother advised me to keep a journal, I did not!

At the end of that year in Washington, Marsh struggled with the decision about whether to stay in the Marines. Anticipating my later vocation as a career counselor, I told him that I believed marriage was to help each other be the best each of us could be, to use our talents as fully as possible. To my way of seeing things, he was only using a limited range of his talents, and I felt stifled in the narrow military life. Still the timing of his leaving the military was inauspicious. The country was in recession, jobs were tight, and furthermore, companies were not interested in hiring Vietnam veterans. After applying for over 80 positions, my husband was finally offered a job at a large bank in New York City.

So our civilian life began. Once both children were in school, I had time to get involved in the community. I joined a new neighbors' club, and became president! I also volunteered in the children's elementary school. My year of volunteer work in the library led to a paid position as an audio-visual aide. At the end of the school year, I responded to a small ad in the local newspaper: "Editor, audiovisual company seeks person familiar with educational materials." Not only was I offered the job, I found a way to work at home on my own time, viewing and evaluating programs and writing entries for the company's catalogue! Flex time, before it had a name!

In a short number of years, I had a series of jobs that introduced me to subjects that have become continuing interests—the changing workplace and workforce, career counseling, mental health, and wellness. From catalog editing, I began writing for *Westchester Magazine* and *Spotlight Magazine,* and then to the editorship of *Mental Health News* for the Mental Health Association of Westchester County (a job that involved producing five issues per year before the computer reduced "cut and paste" to a few keystrokes). This position led in turn to communications consulting for the president of New York Medical College, and then to more writing as a contributing editor on business psychology for *Courier Magazine,* Curtis 1000's corporate magazine.

These writing-intensive jobs overlapped with a time when the discussion of women's liberation was at the center of national life. It was exciting to have work that provided the opportunity to research and write articles about women and psychology. Researching and writing about these changes made me a reporter close to (if not on) the frontlines.

These assignments also led me to think about counseling as a career path. Again, there was a fortuitous element. One of my best story sources—my successor as president of the new neighbors' group—was a career counselor focused on the changing workforce and the related impacts on the workplace and individuals. These changes grabbed my attention and also gave me a mirror on what my husband experienced during his long days at work. I was also interested in the connections between work, health and spiritual well-being.

Over the next few years, we made several more moves as my husband accepted new job opportunities. In the mid-1980s, first our daughter went off to college, soon to be followed by her brother. As the nest emptied, I had more time for research and writing on my growing interest in change in the workplace and the challenges faced by women as they sought to balance the demands of work and family.

Then another fortuitous event. A move to upstate New York led me to a master's program in counseling at the University of Rochester. It felt luxurious to be a student, evaluating past experiences and looking forward. At the same time, two internships provided very practical experience. In one, at a career center, I guided women in focused job searches, testing, and counseling, and was myself the beneficiary of helpful mentoring. In the other, I gained an inside look at one of Rochester's largest employers, Xerox, at a critical time—just after a major workforce reduction. At Xerox, I was part of a team formed by the Manager of Organizational Effectiveness to write a new organizational effectiveness manual that would be accepted by employees who had lost so many co-workers. Writing a manual is one thing, getting employees to take it seriously another. My master's thesis— managing corporate culture change—was one result from this internship. (I like to think that another result of my experience was to give my husband fresh perspective on the large company where he was an operations executive.)

After completing my degree, I was polishing my career counseling résumé, when a new opportunity came along for my husband. With a move back to the New York City area, I thought, why not begin my own counseling practice? New community. New house. Husband in new job. Children settling into their adult lives. I launched Work/Life Decisions.

My goal was a diverse practice. To this end, I did everything from giving YWCA seminars and counseling to displaced housewives, library programs for people considering career changes, corporate relocation for "trailing" spouses (a lot of personal experience to offer on this topic), and corporate outplacement for clients who had lost jobs and needed support finding new positions.

Though my clients were varied, all were experiencing stress. Knowing something about stress myself, I began to incorporate stress management techniques in counseling. My interest in stress and its effects on personal health actually began when I was in high school and happened upon an article in the local paper about a physician named Hans Seyle, whose neuro-endocrine research in the 1930s earned him the title, "father of stress." Dr. Seyle's work indicated that prolonged exposure to intense stress could lead to physiological changes, impacting a person's health and well-being. His research suggested a more holistic approach, one that considered nutrition and exercise, which in turn opened the way to study of mind-body interactions. Even before going into career counseling, I had followed this research and integrated some stress-reduction methods into my own life.

Clients appreciated learning how a stress-management technique, such as awareness of breathing, could help release tension. I also discovered how powerful visualization can be in a group setting. Not long after launching my counseling practice, I gave what I expected would be a medium-size turnout presentation at the town library. A recession was on, and the talk—advertised as "I've Lost My Job, Now What Do I Do?"—drew more than 200 people. After a few preliminaries and some feelings of nervousness myself, I suggested that we close our eyes for a few minutes and try to use our breathing to shift our bodies and minds into a quiet place. I invited everyone to visualize life and career moving forward. After 10 minutes, eyes open, this feeling of group awareness lingered in the air. For me, it was terrific to give so many people a sense of how visualization can prepare a person to control the anxiety associated with looking for a new job. The day after the seminar, the local newspaper carried a full-page article, featuring my picture in action and a detailed account. My experimentation with group visualization validated, I felt new confidence using these techniques, especially in corporate settings.

My career was growing, but so was my husband's. In 1991, Marsh had an opportunity to lead a large bank in another city. We agreed that he should not pass up the position. It meant another move, this one to Boston—a new area for me—from New York, my "home base" since childhood. The move was our third in six years. Even though I believed it was the right thing for us to do, it took a toll on me.

It was ironic that our decision to move to Boston came as I was working with 30 clients whose spouses were being reassigned from Connecticut to Georgia as the result of a corporate headquarters relocation. I told my clients that I might be moving before they did. That turned out to be the case. I was still in the midst of helping these spouses, even as I was unpacking boxes in our new house in Cambridge, meeting new neighbors and new business colleagues, and learning the ropes in a new city. I was able to continue our work by phone and fax. (Fax communications involved walking to and from a copy shop in Harvard Square.)

So much was happening. Gradually, I realized that I wasn't feeling well. My new doctor couldn't determine what was the matter, and suggested the possibility of exhaustion after another move. Meanwhile, I continued with my work and my new role as the wife of a chief executive. Although I came down with a high fever and rash on a trip to Japan, none of the doctors who saw me suggested Lyme disease. Even though I had recently moved from a town in Connecticut where deer trails crisscrossed the woods behind our house, several doctors discounted Lyme disease as a diagnosis and did not order the test.

Months of feeling poorly went by. Luckily, I learned of Dr. Herbert Benson's Mind/Body Institute (then at the Deaconess Hospital, now at Mass General Hospital). I was very familiar with Dr. Benson's famous book, *The Relaxation Response,* so I had no hesitation in registering at the Institute as a patient for a six-week clinical program of healing yoga and meditation. This time my focus was not on stress management, but on using cognitive-behavioral approaches to jump-start my body's self-healing capabilities. My internist, who was at another Boston hospital, monitored me, and through blood test results, could see that my body was responding to the concentrated weeks of the program.

Lyme disease as a diagnosis remained on my mind. By another fortunate coincidence, I learned that Dr. Allan Steere, who had discovered the disease when he was at Yale-New Haven Hospital, was giving grand rounds at the Deaconess Hospital. Only a few slides into his presentation, I KNEW that what I had was Lyme disease. Within several weeks of Dr. Steer's talk, I was diagnosed with late Lyme disease, accepted into his research program, and started treatment with the appropriate antibiotic.

I was fortunate that my case of Lyme disease responded to the antibiotic. Even when I was on the road to recovery, I continued with the program at the Mind/Body Institute, and post-program, adopted mind/body exercises at home. I also began meditation courses and workshops, some taught by Jon Kabat-Zinn, the MIT-trained microbiologist, who has dedicated himself to bringing mindfulness to the mainstream of medicine and society. Working to recover, I was expanding my horizons, too.

Once again, a difficult experience—suffering with undiagnosed Lyme disease for months at the time of our move, when my symptoms were dismissed as stress-related—led to an opportunity. After my recovery, Dr. Benson asked if I would help develop seminars for a corporate and workplace program at the Mind/Body Institute. As a consultant to the Institute, I was able to contribute my career counseling experience and at the same time learn so much about the connections between stress and illness and relaxation and healing.

Another opportunity came to me through my husband's new position. He had to travel widely on business, and so I accompanied him on many trips. As a spouse, my schedule was freer than his, and allowed me to explore and expand my acquaintance with other religions and cultures, especially in Asia. (In fact, our first business trip abroad was the one on which I had unknowingly been acutely ill with Lyme disease.) These travels showed me that there were more connections than differences beyond the way things looked in Buddhist temples and the Christian churches. (Ironically, our first church in Westchester County was a pagoda-shaped Maryknoll center for Catholic missionaries.) Icons and images may be specific to particular cultures, but parallels between the age-old questions and searches for meaning and the afterlife are there, too.

Increasingly, Boston came to feel like home. Living nestled in an academic neighborhood was comfortable, a bit freer than in the corporate suburbs outside of New York City. A spirit of inquiry is in the Cambridge air, and I decided to give myself the permission to swing wider and differently in my spiritual journey. Cambridge offers proximity to maybe a dozen centers where one can explore and study Buddhist philosophy. Several are within walking distance of my home. I began to meditate every day. Gradually over time, meditation became more and more natural, and I integrated it into my prayer life.

Through these years of travel and study, my spirituality became more connected to my relationship with God. So often, I happened on a book or a conversation that helped me respond to life's challenges. My growth helped me handle many changes: the death of our four parents, my mother—two days after my daughter's wedding, and my mother-in-law—the day after our son's graduate school graduation. Not many years later, my daughter-in-law-to-be, lost her mother to cancer one week before the wedding. Those happy, sad twins repeating, reminding that life is bittersweet. On September 11, 2001, I happened to be in New York City visiting my daughter and her two young children. Experiencing the horror of the attacks, while maintaining an outward calm in front of my young grandchildren, brought back intense memories of my life as a young mother with a husband serving in Vietnam.

Gradually, I worked with fewer career-counseling clients. The impact of the Internet on résumé-writing, researching jobs and applying online changed the way that client and counselor work together. In the meantime, my interest in mind/body expanded to mind/body/spirit. Although I continue to be interested in workforce issues, I decided to close my private practice in 2004.

The past 15 years have been an exciting time for those who seek to understand the inter-relationships of mind, body, and spirit. In 1995, the Mind/Body Institute held its first conference on spirituality and healing. Sponsored by Harvard Medical School, the conference brought together physicians and nurses in mainstream medicine, ministers, priests, Sufis, rabbis, Christian Scientists, yoga teachers—a wide spectrum of people, all coming together to explore health in a holistic way. Since then, such conferences have drawn more and more interest and participation.

Practices which were once far out on the "alternative" spectrum—acupuncture, acupressure, yoga, reiki, pilates—have multiplied and are increasingly seen as complementary to traditional medicine. In early 2009, the Institute of Medicine held a "summit" in

Washington on Integrative Medicine—defined as health care that addresses the mental, physical and emotional aspects of the healing process—for improved patient-centered care and the nation's health. I was fortunate to attend.

Research in neuroscience has exploded, and neuroscientists are beginning to understand not only how the brain works, but also how mind, body and spirit work together. The Dalai Lama was an early proponent of such research, believing that meditation has an important effect on health. Some of the first evidence was drawn from measurement of brainwaves, blood pressure and heart rates of Tibetan monks at Dharamsala, India. Research on the neuroscience of meditation has led to studies of "neuroplasticity"—the brain's ability to rewire itself. The assumption that old brain cells die, never to be replaced, has turned out to be wrong. The search is on for what can change the brain. Some neuroscientists are also asking, "Are we wired for God?"

Spiritual leaders have been watching these developments as they open dialogues with each other. One exemplar is Father Thomas Keating, who founded the Centering Prayer movement. For nearly 30 years, he has convened annual meetings, bringing together practitioners from the major religions—Judaism, Christianity, Islam, Hinduism, Buddhism, Baha'i Faith, Native American. Coming together, adherents of these varied religions and practices use their methods of concentration, meditation and prayer to develop respect and cooperation across peoples and countries. Through interfaith communication, they seek to create a more just and peaceful world. Father Keating and others have given the word "ecumenism" a new depth of meaning. Such efforts to promote understanding inspire me.

My grandchildren—who now all live within a mile of my home—have the power to fill me with pure love and joy. As they grow older, and my husband and I do too, my perspective is shifting again. I walk the journey aware of the turns, some after long stretches, some shorter but always trying to keep the center in view. As long as I keep God's love as my center, I am steadied in my path with its surprises, sadness, and joy. It is in this spirit that I offer Living Lines.

A Note for Readers

After years of writing and collecting reflections, I began to feel the urge to share the ones that have been "lifelines" to me. I thought of them as "lifelines" for they gave me strength and perspective at challenging times. My urge to share strengthened as I meditated on my lifelines in the course of normal days. At the same time, my internal name "lifelines" morphed into "living lines." As I began to select and edit reflections for this book, they became "Living Lines"—capitalized. Though my collecting began very privately, the capital Ls reflect my decision to share.

Some of the Living Lines are my own words; others are reflections written by others. Where the lines are mine, I have included a note on the situation that led me to them. Where a reflection is another author's, I have also included a biographical note. The process of adding these notes strengthened my desire to share. It is humbling to mix my own words with those of saints, physicians, and authors, whose words are already well known. Mine may not match the eloquence of theirs, but I feel a kinship with them nonetheless. The questions and the search for answers are the same, and so is the desire to share.

It is my hope that these Living Lines will speak to my friends and others. These pages can be approached in different ways. In the first section are Living Lines that are my touchstones. They are questions that I pose to myself, if not each day, then regularly. Though our interests and needs may vary, we all can benefit from taking time to listen to our inner selves. Following the first section, the Living Lines are divided into themes—for example, relationships, stress, coping, healing, and gratitude—for reflection. Some readers may prefer picking among themes, and have more interest in some than others. Another approach is simply to open the book and find a page with a Living Line that speaks to you in the moment.

As those who read Living Lines will realize, books have been my comforts, guides, inspirations. For me, "biblio-therapy" is a way of gaining perspective on where I have been and what may lie ahead. There are times when I open myself to the process of thinking, letting subjects—people, books just read, problems, accomplishments—come into my mind in no particular order. My response is often to go to the library or a bookstore or my own library shelves, and ask myself whether there is something there for me. It is amazing how many times I am drawn to a shelf and find a book that illuminates a concern and gives me focus.

Spiritual searching has been a preoccupation of writers since ancient times. One could spend a lifetime reading and studying such books. I hope that this modest book will allow you to select readings from this vast assortment that will be the most meaningful to you. And perhaps my practice of writing short reflections while reading will appeal to you. For me, such writing is a way of entering into a personal dialogue with the author. As I read, when something catches my attention or speaks very directly to me, I stop to reflect. Sometimes, I underline and continue reading. Other times, I reread a passage several times, commit the thought to memory, and stop there. Occasionally, I copy the words verbatim; other times, I write something of my own. My library is full of books with pages marked by pieces of paper, placed for later reference. This book is my way of sharing all those places where I have stopped and found a Living Line.

Three Questions

How are you?

"Hello, how are you?" We ask, or are asked, this question throughout the day, by friends, store associates, business colleagues, even by computer voices. Is this question really posed in expectation of an answer? Here, I am earnest in asking, "How are you?"

Who are you?

Are you truly living your life? Or are you trying to be someone else? So, "Who are you?"

Are you living in fullness?

What do these words mean? How does it feel to live in fullness? For me, this question means to live in a way that engages mind, body, and spirit. And on those days when all your powers of physical, mental and spiritual concentration are in sync, you will know what it is to "live in fullness."

How are you? Who are you?
Are you living in fullness?

I try to hold these questions in my mind (and heart) and to consider them anew each day. The Living Lines in this book are reflections that have given me insights into my three core questions. Some reflections rephrase them. Others suggest answers. This book is my invitation to my friends and others to join me in turning over these questions, and in doing so, to pursue the goal of living in fullness, engaging mind, body, and spirit.

Meaning of Life

Mary Oliver, "The Summer Day," *New and Selected Poems: Volume One* (Boston: Beacon Press, 1992), p. 84

Poet Mary Oliver (1935–) draws inspiration from close observation of the natural world in the tradition of Thoreau, Whitman and Dickinson. A native of Ohio, she considers New England landscapes, especially the woods and fields of Provincetown, with the appraising eye of an adopted daughter. She has won numerous awards and honors, including the 1984 Pulitzer Prize in Poetry for *American Primitive*.

I have read that Mary Oliver's neighbors know her as much for her daily walks as for being found standing still, entranced. Ms. Oliver's poems are meditations on the wonders of life, invitations to stop and consider the divinity around us and in us.

The Summer Day

Who made the world?
Who made the swan, and the black bear?
Who made the grasshopper?
This grasshopper, I mean—
the one who has flung herself out of the grass,
the one who is eating sugar out of my hand,
who is moving her jaws back and forth instead of up and down—
who is gazing around with her enormous and complicated eyes.
Now she lifts her pale forearms and thoroughly washes her face.
Now she snaps her wings open, and floats away.
I don't know exactly what a prayer is.
I do know how to pay attention, how to fall down
into the grass, how to kneel down in the grass,
how to be idle and blessed, how to stroll through the fields,
which is what I have been doing all day.
Tell me, what else should I have done?
Doesn't everything die at last, and too soon?
Tell me, what is it you plan to do
with your one wild and precious life?

—Mary Oliver

Robert J. Wicks, *Riding the Dragon: Ten Lessons for Inner Strength in Challenging Times* (Notre Dame, Indiana: Sorin Books, 2003), pp. 90–91

Professor of Pastoral Counseling at Loyola University in Maryland, Robert Wicks is a clinical psychologist whose research is focused on handling "secondary stress"—sometimes described as "compassion fatigue" or even vicarious post-traumatic stress disorder—experienced by relief workers, nurses, physicians and other health professionals who care for others. Educated in the Jesuit tradition, Dr. Wicks's writing integrates psychology and spirituality and draws from his study of Western and Eastern religions. In *Riding the Dragon*, he offers lessons from his clinical work to a lay audience. His book is full of tips on how to "ride" the dragons—the forces that challenge us—rather than trying to slay or vanquish them.

Too often in an effort to be a better person,
we only wind up
trying to be another person—
a sure recipe for continued failure
and a sense of "lostness."

—Robert J. Wicks

The word "lostness" is awkward, yet provocative, intended to make the reader think. How do I know when I am truly being myself, not the reflection of someone I may be trying to be or someone others are expecting? Wicks suggests that trying to be someone else is futile, and will lead to a sense of being lost. When I am myself—really present in the moment, I don't feel lost, even though I might be in an uncomfortable or unpleasant situation. Being myself does not mean that I will never feel uncomfortable.

Agnes de Mille, *And Promenade Home* (Boston: An Atlantic Monthly Press Book, Little, Brown and Company, 1958), p. 190

Dancer and choreographer, Agnes de Mille (1905–1993) was born into a theatrical family. (Her grandfather and father were playwrights and her uncle was Cecil B. DeMille.) As a young girl, she formed the determination to be a dancer and then devoted herself to that goal. Despite the occasional positive review, she was nearly 40 before she found widespread acclaim, first at the American Ballet Theatre with her uniquely American work *Rodeo,* and then as the choreographer of Rodgers and Hammerstein's *Oklahoma!* Along with this new fame, Agnes de Mille also came to be recognized as a witty writer and engaging speaker-performer, an ambassador for the arts. Though she suffered a life-altering cerebral hemorrhage at the age of 70, she applied her willpower to rehabilitation, and continued to compose and write (learning to use her left hand in the process). The PBS *Great Performances: Dance in America* retrospective on de Mille's career was aptly titled "Agnes: The Indomitable De Mille."

Living is a form of not being sure, of not knowing what next or how. The artist…never entirely knows. He guesses. And he may be wrong. …One leaps in the dark.

—Agnes de Mille

To me, Agnes de Mille suggests that we should think of ourselves as "artists," creating our lives, not being afraid to take some risks. We may not be painters or poets or dancers, but we are the authors—creators—of our own lives. Leaps in the dark—risks—must sometimes be taken.

Joseph Campbell, with Bill Moyers; Betty Sue Flowers, ed., *The Power of Myth* (New York: Doubleday, A Division of Bantam Doubleday Dell Publishing Group, 1988), p. 3

Raised a Catholic, Joseph Campbell (1904–1987) became fascinated by mythology at an early age. He was not afraid to take risks or, at least, to veer from the conventional path. Late in life, his writings on comparative mythology and comparative religion became best sellers thanks to his PBS series with Bill Moyers. Although Campbell's philosophy is sometimes summarized as "Follow your bliss," this phrase doesn't do justice to the breadth of his work. To read Campbell is to search with him for the transcendent truths of the world's mythologies and the responses of the 20th-century's preeminent intellectuals, writers, and artists.

People say that what we're all seeking is a meaning for life.
I don't think that's what we're really seeking.
I think that what we're seeking is an experience of being alive, so that
our life experiences on the purely physical plane will have resonances
within our innermost being and reality,
so that we can actually feel the rapture of being alive.

—Joseph Campbell

To me, Joseph Campbell's words explain the shorthand phrase "being in the moment."
Though we may seem far removed from the drama of Greek myth or Arthurian legend,
Campbell reminds us to be open to the adventure and truth in life.

The Society of Saint John the Evangelist North American Congregation, "Obedience in Practice," *The Rule of the Society of Saint John the Evangelist* (Cambridge, Massachusetts: Cowley Publications, 1997), p. 26

A monastery belonging to this Anglican religious order for men is just a short walk from my own home. Their chapel is open to the community as a sanctuary for daily prayer and reflection.

"God has called us to be active co-creators in Christ,
not passive recipients of external instructions."

—The Society of Saint John the Evangelist

The members of the Society of St. John the Evangelist live under a rule of life and make monastic vows of poverty, celibacy, and obedience in enduring fellowship. However, their vows do not require separation from the world. Indeed, in their ministries and at home, the brothers aim "above all" to be "Men of the Moment," responsive to "the call of God and the needs of our world in the present day."

Born in Asia Minor to a Greek family, St. Irenaeus (second century C.E.) became Bishop of Lugdunum in Gaul (now Lyon, France). Recognized as a saint in both the Eastern and Western Church, Irenaeus was a central figure in the doctrinal debates that shaped Christianity. Though the debates of the second century may seem arcane today, St. Irenaeus' essential message was nonetheless a simple one, namely, that human beings are created in the image of God, and as such, will find God in their very humanity.

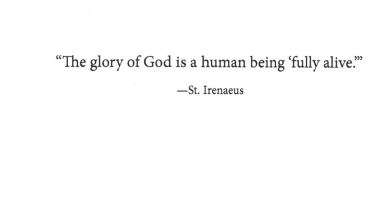

"The glory of God is a human being 'fully alive.'"

—St. Irenaeus

The words of St. Irenaeus have circulated in sermons for 1,800 years. The concept of "living in the moment" is not a new one!

Who am I bringing
to the moment?

Sometimes I rephrase the "Who am I?" question to this one. We all have many roles in our lives, and we often move in and out of them automatically. Especially on busy days, I find it helpful to take a quiet moment and listen for "me." I ask myself, "Is there consistency in my various me's?"

I want to wear my own shoes as long as they fit!

Some days my shoes feel like they fit; other days, my feet feel constricted. Just like shoe sizes, one's comfort zone does not stay constant. Sometimes we are pushed to explore new experiences. And so I ask myself, do I feel constrained inside? Do I need to move beyond my comfort zone to grow?

Martha Graham, as recalled by Agnes de Mille in *Martha, The Life and Work of Martha Graham* (New York: Random House, 1991), p. 264

Martha Graham (1894–1991) was a pioneer of dance and choreography—pushing the boundaries of both from the 1920s on. She gave these words of advice to her younger contemporary Agnes de Mille, at a time when her friend was unsettled by sudden success after years of work that she thought good, even better, but that had received little attention. When Agnes expressed doubts about her scale of values, Martha exhorted her to continue, to have faith, and not to sit in judgment of herself.

A neighbor gave me these words and I keep them over my desk. So, as I sit down at my computer in the morning, I read Martha Graham's wise counsel to her friend Agnes de Mille. She encourages me, especially on the days when what I am doing doesn't seem to be making a contribution or of much value. Martha Graham reminds me, I should not judge myself. My job is to be open to possibility.

There is a vitality, a life force, an energy, a quickening
that is translated through you into action,
and because there is only one of you in all of time,
this expression is unique.
And if you block it,
it will never exist through any other medium and it will be lost.
The world will not have it.
It is not your business to determine how good it is
nor how valuable
nor how it compares with other expressions.
It is your business to keep it yours clearly and directly,
to keep the channel open.

—Martha Graham

Rabbi Irwin Kula, *Yearnings: Embracing the Sacred Messiness of Life* (New York: Hyperion Books, 2006), p. 45

Rabbi Irwin Kula brings Jewish wisdom to modern life and relationships. An eighth-generation rabbi, he is also a philosophy Ph.D. with a radio talk show and a blog. Host of a public television series and frequent guest on popular shows, Rabbi Kula uses his gift for communicating ideas to reach out across religions.

The ability to live with seeming contradictions,
and the ambivalence and tension these contradictions create,
is what gives rise to wisdom.
The messes are the point.

—Rabbi Irwin Kula

Rabbi Kula's Yearnings *is full of insightful comments. After reading it, I asked my friend Faye Kimerling if she knew of it. She said yes. Months later, on rereading a talk that she gave to her congregation on Yom Kippur, I realized that she had quoted Rabbi Kula. The passage above is the one that she chose. Rabbi Kula's message reassures us that not all questions can—or should be—answered. Sometimes we must accept that certain things are unknowable, and so must live with the resulting questions. To do so can enlarge the scope of what is possible.*

Jacqueline Novogratz, "Dignity Is More Important Than Wealth—A Universal Truth," Blog posted March 19, 2010

Jacqueline Novogratz (1962–) is the founder of Acumen, a nonprofit venture fund that provides financing for entrepreneurial projects in South Asia and East Africa. Since 2001, the fund has provided grants of philanthropic capital directly to enterprises that deliver critical goods and services (like clean drinking water and affordable health care) along with management support and "moral" imagination. In doing so, Acumen aims to change the lives of large numbers of poor people.

Ms. Novogratz's recent book, *The Blue Sweater: Bridging the Gap Between Rich and Poor in an Interconnected World,* is the story of how she left a career in traditional investment banking for a mission as a social investor.

Since founding Acumen, Ms. Novogratz has made dignity her core message. Recently, she met a Pakistani woman, who told her: "…self-respect is more important than wealth." Hearing these words from this heroic woman, Ms. Novogratz was struck once again by how much all peoples have in common regardless of class, ethnicity or religion.

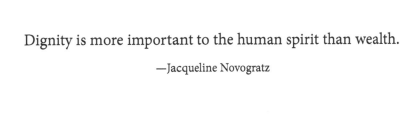

Dignity is more important to the human spirit than wealth.

—Jacqueline Novogratz

Eleven years after donating a once-treasured blue sweater to a Goodwill store in Virginia, Jacqueline Novogratz was jogging in Kigali, the capital of Rwanda, when she saw a skinny 10-year-old boy wearing her sweater! Running to him and communicating by signs, she turned down the collar and saw her name on the tag! That stunning discovery led Ms. Novogratz to realize how interconnected we are—that what we do or don't do can affect people we may never meet.

Rainer Maria Rilke, *Letters to a Young Poet,* translated by Stephen Mitchell (New York: Modern Library, A Division of Random House, 2001), p. 34

One of Germany's best-known poets, Rainer Maria Rilke (1875–1926) has continued to be discovered and appreciated by new generations. Born to a minority German family in Prague (then in the Austro-Hungarian Empire), Rilke had a difficult childhood as the only child of incompatible parents and a military-school education unsuited to his nature. His biography is a romantic one: youthful relationship with an older married woman (an intimate of Nietzsche and friend of Freud), who encouraged him in his determination to write poetry, introduced him to the wider world, and remained a confidant; brief settling in an artists' colony in northern Germany where he married another artist (though he departed upon the birth of a child, the marriage continued); wanderings across Europe, including Russia, where he was introduced to Tolstoy, and Paris, where he was associated with (and influenced by) Rodin; conscription in the Austrian army during World War I; and finally refuge in Switzerland.

Rilke was fortunate in the support of patrons who appreciated his gifts. Restless by nature, he went through periods of creative crisis when he wrote little, and then bursts of creativity, reportedly setting down poems with great speed. Though he fell away from the Catholic Church (and the notion of a personal God) as a young man, he continued to search for spiritual meaning and goodness—a search that is still much quoted today.

Rilke never met the young man to whom these letters were addressed. Though he customarily answered letters from admirers, Rilke perhaps took extra care with his replies to the young poet, who was a student at a military school where he had spent his own early teenage years. Rilke himself was only 27—just nine years older than his correspondent—when the exchange began. The correspondence—10 letters in all—spanned nearly six years in time, early 1903 to late 1908, and many miles and varied residences in France, Italy, Germany, and Sweden. The letters—a mediation on solitude, creativity and love—were published by the "young poet," Franz Xaver Kappus, in 1929, three years after Rilke's death. On reading *Letters to a Young Poet,* one can almost feel Rilke composing, choosing his words, and then imagine the feelings of the young poet upon reading them.

…have patience with everything unresolved in your heart and…
try to love *the questions themselves*
as if they were locked rooms or books written
in a very foreign language.
Don't search for the answers, which could not be given to you now,
because you would not be able to live them.
And the point is, to live everything.
Live the questions now.
Perhaps then, someday far in the future,
you will gradually, without even noticing it,
live your way into the answer.

—Rainer Maria Rilke

Like artists, we must find a meaningful question or problem to solve in order to give focus to our work and lives. How difficult it can be to identify one's central question and then live it without a schedule for answers. The challenge is to let go—experience the process and trust that answers will come.

Quotations as drawn from Margaret Silf's essay, "The Road to Emmaus," *America,* March 17, 2008

An English writer, Ms. Silf's central topic is Christian spirituality and her focus is on making it accessible for people with no theological background. In columns for *America,* the Catholic weekly, she takes an experiential approach, drawing connections between Christian teachings and the choices of everyday living.

As Albert Einstein reportedly once said,
"You will never solve a problem with the same mind-set that created it."
Or as a non-physicist put Einstein's maxim:
"If you always think what you always thought,
you will always do what you always did and
you will always get what you always got."

This reflection came to me courtesy of a column by a favorite writer, Margaret Silf. In a revealing essay, she tells the story of a chance meeting with another woman—whose childhood paralleled hers—at the opening of a homeless center in the city where she had grown up. While Ms. Silf had escaped early thanks to a college prep school, the other woman had not been so lucky, but eventually salvaged her life. This woman, also named Margaret, summarized her empirically derived philosophy in the three lines above. The two Margarets enjoyed a laugh at the similarity to Einstein's famous maxim. Speaking of which, was Einstein's mind more powerful than other physicists of his time? Or was he simply better at reframing problems in a way that led him to solutions?

See what is.
The tape playing in the back of our minds
often distracts us from
what is right in front of us.

Taken together, "see what is" are three challenging words. I pause several times a day to check whether the tape in my mind is related to what is right in front of me.

I no longer make a plan for myself
but respond to the things in my life
that are part of a pattern or a plan
I cannot see.

This reflection became my mantra and my prayer when—after moving for the third time in six years, I realized that I needed to take a break, learn to be "quiet," so I could "hear." With so many moves, I was making a new home, finding work, working, traveling with my husband on business. There was so much to do in a day, a week, a month. I needed to find perspective. On the surface, these words may sound passive, but they remind me to strive for an active awareness. While I may not be in control of events, I can be ready to respond.

Reese Witherspoon, channeling June Carter Cash in her acceptance speech for the Academy Award for Best Actress in a Lead Role in *Walk the Line,* 78th Academy Awards, March 5, 2006

In her Academy Award speech, Ms. Witherspoon recalled that when June Carter Cash was asked how she was doing, she would reply, "I'm just tryin' to matter…" The actress noted that she knew what June meant, adding about herself, "I'm just tryin' to matter and live a good life, and make work that means something to somebody…"

Reese Witherspoon won her first lead role in a major film as a 15-year-old in 1991, and was recognized early for her comedic gifts. In *Walk the Line,* Ms. Witherspoon showed her dramatic range, in a challenging role that even required her to sing before a live audience. She saw the compassion in June Carter Cash's personality, and succeeded in projecting it. As for acting, Ms. Witherspoon has said it is a "career," but just one aspect of her life. The mother of two children, Ms. Witherspoon has been an advocate for children and women's health issues.

"I'm just tryin' to matter
and live a good life,
and make work that means something to somebody..."

—Reese Witherspoon

Not many of us work in fields where awards are given each year. Sometimes, we don't see that our lives matter. But the discipline that it takes to keep at it, without seeing the results, is surely the foundation for a meaningful life.

When I jotted these lines from Ms. Witherspoon's speech, I didn't know much about her biography. In verifying her words, I learned that, like quite few of the authors and artists whom I've quoted in these Living Lines, Reese Witherspoon counts a line of ministers among her forebears.

We spend much more time
being Human Doers
than Human Beings.

I overheard a woman make this observation to her neighbor in line at the post office years ago. These words remind me how wonderful it is to BE. The balance between doing and being seems to be shifting in favor of being as more people take up meditation, practice yoga, and make time for retreats from busy lives.

Sometimes I have the opportunity
to do something,
go somewhere,
or meet someone.

At another time in my life,
I might have
given my eye teeth
for these opportunities.

But then I realize
that this time is
not the right time.

Timing is everything, so people say. How much my perspective and desires have changed over time. I am sometimes surprised that I don't leap at opportunities that would have once been irresistible.

St. Abba Macarius, as quoted by Robert Wicks in *Riding the Dragon: Ten Lessons for Inner Strength in Challenging Times* (Notre Dame, Indiana: Sorin Books, 2003), p. 94

St. Macarius (c. 300–390) was a founding father of monasticism, one of the desert fathers—the first Christian hermits—who sought salvation in the solitude and asceticism of the deserts of the Middle East in the fourth century. Disciples often appealed to these men for spiritual guidance. The resulting stories and sayings were recorded, and have come down to us today in translation as "Sayings of the Fathers of the Desert."

Don't try to understand everything—
take on board as much as you can and try to make it work for you.
Then the things that are hidden will be made clear to you.

—St. Abba Macarius

The words of St. Macarius, who lived 60 years of his life in a desert monastery, resonate with me. Although we live in an information age with the assumption that we can find out all we need to know, almost instantaneously, life still has its mysteries, with much that is hidden. At times, I can barely see one step in front of me, let alone the whole path. When the path seems dark, the image of this ancient desert monk reminds me to go step by step and to have faith that the lines of the path will be revealed.

Johann Wolfgang von Goethe, *Faust, Part I,* Faust and Mephistopheles in the Study

Novelist, dramatist, poet, and philosopher, Johann Wolfgang von Goethe (1749–1832) is generally considered the most important writer in the German language. Truly a polymath, Goethe's works had an enormous influence on the course of literature and philosophy. His great two-part work, *Faust,* was written over many years (the earliest version drafted in his 20s and *Part II* being published posthumously) and has the power of a gathering wisdom.

Just trust yourself,
and then you will know how to live.

—Johann Wolfgang von Goethe

These words of Goethe's are widely cited without reference to their textual source. It gave me pause to go to the play, and find that they are words of seductive reassurance, spoken by Mephistopheles to Faust. Though Mephistopheles is the devil's agent, his advice speaks a truth—second-guessing ourselves, not trusting our instincts, can make us too self-conscious to live fully.

The amount of time and energy
we spend trying to figure out our lives
might be better spent in living.
We build self-confidence by living
rather than thinking about it.

Planning is certainly important, but thinking about living too much keeps us from experiencing it. Occasionally, I realize that I am spending more time organizing to do something than if I just went ahead and did it!

"Rise to the occasion."
My mother often said that.

Looking back over decades, I see that I did rise to the occasion, even when I thought I could not. When I was young, women's liberation led to a standard of being superwoman. And so, I continued a pattern—begun in childhood—of attempting to rise to the occasion. Looking back at decades of unexpected occasions, I realize there might have been some that weren't my responsibility. With experience, I have learned to make sure an occasion requires my energies before I go out and meet it.

Buddha, from Chapter I, "The Twin-Verses" of *The Dhammapada* in *The Sacred Books of the East*, 1881

Buddha, (c. 563–483 B.C.E.), Siddhattha Gotama, the spiritual teacher, who came to be known as Buddha or the Awakened One, lived in the northeast of the Indian subcontinent. Accounts of his life, discourses, and monastic rules are believed by Buddhists to have been summarized after his death and memorized by his followers. Collections of teachings attributed to Buddha—like this one—were passed down by oral tradition, and only committed to writing 400 years after his death. Recorded in Ceylon a century before Christ, *The Dhammapada* is a collection of sayings that summarize the Buddha's understanding of the foundation of truth.

All that we are is the result of what we have thought:
it is founded on our thoughts,
it is made up of our thoughts.
If a man speaks or acts with an evil thought,
pain follows him,
as the wheel follows the foot of the ox that draws the carriage.

All that we are is the result of what we have thought:
it is founded on our thoughts,
it is made up of our thoughts.
If a man speaks or acts with a pure thought,
happiness follows him,
like a shadow that never leaves him.

—Buddha

A simple description of what is called "karma."

Jon Kabat-Zinn, *Wherever You Go, There You Are, Mindfulness Meditation in Everyday Life* (New York: Hyperion, 1994), pp. 220–21

Trained as microbiologist at MIT, Dr. Kabat-Zinn has devoted his career to bringing mindfulness into the mainstream of medical practice. The author of numerous scientific papers on the clinical applications of mindfulness in medicine and health care, he has also written or co-written a list of bestsellers for general audiences. He is a professor emeritus at the University of Massachusetts Medical School, where he founded the stress reduction clinic, the first such academic program in the world. In addition to his research on the use of mindfulness meditation in medicine, Dr. Kabat-Zinn has explored how such practices may offer wider social benefits when applied in the workplace, schools, prisons, and competitive sports.

My copy of Dr. Kabat-Zinn's book is loose on the seams and the pages slip out. It is a wonderful, perspective-giving book for either a beginning meditator or someone who has practiced for a long time. You do not need to be a Buddhist to practice mindfulness; Dr. Kabat-Zinn describes the essence of mindfulness meditation, so that it may be of practical benefit to anyone.

...when we speak of a person's karma,
it means the sum total of the person's direction in life and
the tenor of the things that occur around that person,
caused by antecedent conditions, actions, thoughts, feelings,
sense impressions, desires...
It is always possible to change your karma.
...Here's how mindfulness changes karma.
When you sit [in mindfulness],
you are not allowing your impulses to translate into action...
Looking at them, you quickly see that [impulses in the mind]
...are not you but just thinking,
and that you do not have to be ruled by them
...and in doing so [mindfulness] unchains us, frees us,
and opens up new directions for us
through the moments we call life.
Without mindfulness,
we are all too easily stuck in the momentum coming out of the past,
with no clue to our own imprisonment, and no way out.

—Jon Kabat-Zinn

Meaning of Life

Jon Kabat-Zinn, *Wherever You Go There You Are,* 10th Anniversary Edition, p. 273

Years ago, I discovered Dr. Jon Kabat-Zinn's book, Wherever You Go, There You Are, *at a meditation seminar, and I have been reading and recommending the book ever since. My copy of the 10th anniversary edition, given to me by the author, is almost as well used as my original.*

...you are already perfect.
We all are.
Perfectly what we are,
including all the imperfections and inadequacies
The question is:
can we be with it?
Can we sit with it?
Can we know it?
Can we embrace our own wholeness
and embody it,
here,
where we already are,
in the very situations, good, bad, ugly, lost,
confusing, heart-rending,
terrifying, and painful,
that we find ourselves in?
...Can we realize that wherever we go,
there we are and
that this "there" is always "here"
and so requires at least acknowledgment
and perhaps a degree of acceptance of what is,
however it is,
because it already is?
Can we grow into ourselves
in our fullness
and live our precious and fleeting lives
more wisely?

—Jon Kabat-Zinn

Sue Monk Kidd, *When the Heart Waits: Spiritual Direction for Life's Sacred Questions* (San Francisco: Harper & Row, 1990), p. 52

When the Heart Waits is more than a sharing of one woman's personal story of midlife questioning. Sue Monk Kidd had undertaken an earlier spiritual quest in the hope of finding a "more contemplative way of being in the world." Having already read and reflected deeply, her midlife-crisis book is an introduction to a literature of spiritual seekers as far back to the Middle Ages. She brings the poetry of others to the page and then adds her own. Ms. Kidd's book is truly a spiritual classic.

God guides us on the long way round.
And sometimes that means winding through a dark wood.
It doesn't mean we're lost, however. The darkness is part of the trip.
Too many of us panic in the dark.
We don't understand that it's a holy dark and that the idea is to
surrender to it and journey through to real light.

—Sue Monk Kidd

Sue Monk Kidd's book speaks of her own spiritual crisis. Her beautiful words have stayed with me like a prayer. (In fact, I borrowed her phrase—"the long way round"— as a title for my introduction.) It is interesting that Ms. Kidd wrote her first novel, The Secret Life of Bees, *more than a decade after* When the Heart Waits. *Even with the success of that autobiographical book, could she have foreseen the success of her first novel, which became an "overnight" bestseller and then a Hollywood movie?*

Thanks to a conversation with my friend LuAnn Polk, who introduced me to labyrinths and Lauren Artress's book *Walking a Sacred Path: Rediscovering the Labyrinth as a Spiritual Practice.*

Uncharted paths—do those words go together?
It's as if our eyes are on the back of our heads
so we can see where we've come from.
Can we see where we're going?
If we walked backward,
would we then see the path ahead?
A puzzle.

Life—looked at in reverse—seems to show us what we needed to find the place where we are now. Those steps that seemed like zigs and zags at the time can, in retrospect, reveal that we took the most direct path after all.

The longer I live,
the more I learn not to measure in percentages
how I am doing or what I've accomplished.
Life is not a line, easily measured.
Increasingly, I see it as a circle,
where past weaves into present and
the present illuminates the past,
round and round.

We all fail.
We should all take risks anyway.

Where did I ever get the notion that I could do things without making mistakes? Life is a risk and if I don't keep trying, regardless of not doing well or failing, I won't learn or become better at something. I am growing in my understanding that when someone does something seemingly without effort it is the result of practice, practice, practice.

Louis Pasteur, Lecture at University of Lille, 1854

Born to a humble line of tanners, Louis Pasteur (1822–1895) became a revered chemist and microbiologist. His accomplishments included the development of a process of killing bacteria and molds present in milk, wine and beer; advances in immunology, including a vaccine for rabies; foundational work in germ theory and bacteriology, which reduced mortality of women from puerperal fever and encouraged the development of antiseptic measures in surgery.

A patient experimental scientist, Pasteur was also a spiritual man. Although three of his five children died before reaching adulthood (two from typhoid), their deaths did not cause him to lose faith. Rather, they spurred him to look for cures to disease. For Pasteur, the laboratory was a sacred domain where he stood amazed at the work of "the Creator." Indeed, Pasteur said, "I pray while I am engaged at my work in the laboratory." Sir William Osler (also quoted in Living Lines) remembered Pasteur's creed thus, "I see everywhere the inevitable expression of the Infinite in the world; through it the supernatural is at the bottom of every heart."

In the field of observation, chance favors only the prepared mind.

—Louis Pasteur

We cannot always see where we are going until we get there. Sometimes we are preparing for something we haven't even set as a goal.

Alexander Pope (1688–1744), *An Essay on Criticism*, 1709

Pope's words, which referred to literary critics, have been quoted with more or less precision by authors from Edmund Burke to Thomas Hardy, E.M. Forster and James Joyce as well as in song by artists, including Frank Sinatra, Elvis Presley, Ricky Nelson, among many others. It is interesting to note that Pope was born a Catholic, and held to this faith even though in doing so he was barred from public office and employment.

Fools rush in
where angels
fear to tread.

—Alexander Pope

My interpretation of Pope's aphorism: A risk taker sometimes lives more fully than an angel who follows all the rules.

Meaning of Life

Seek and ye shall find;
but it can take a damn long time!

Priorities

These words have been quoted in motivational writing, both psychological and religious, as Stevenson's since the 1880s, but without reference to the actual source. (They may be the inspiration for the early 20th century American proverb—"the best things in life are free.")

Plagued by ill health from childhood, Robert Louis Stevenson (1850–1894)—Scottish essayist, poet, novelist, traveler and travel writer—traveled and wrote almost ceaselessly. His search for a more salubrious climate took him to France and America, and ultimately to Samoa in the South Pacific, where he died at the age of 44. A precocious storyteller and writer, Stevenson absorbed childhood experiences—the frightening tales and Bible-reading of his sternly Presbyterian nurse; visits to lighthouses with his father, who came from a line of lighthouse engineers; and the sermons of his maternal grandfather, a Church of Scotland minister—and turned them into grist for his romantic adventures.

Though best known now as the author of children's books such as *Treasure Island* and *Kidnapped*, Stevenson also produced nonfiction that recorded his life's journeys and offered shrewd observations of human nature. A friend of Henry James, Stevenson influenced and was admired by such later masters as Joseph Conrad and Vladimir Nabokov.

The best things are nearest:
Breath in your nostrils, light in your eyes,
flowers at your feet, duties at your hand,
the path of God just before you.
Then do not grasp at the stars,
but do life's plain, common work as it comes,
certain that daily duties and daily bread are the sweetest things of life.

—Attributed to Robert Louis Stevenson

Robert Louis Stevenson's famous adventure novels read almost like screenplays, yet were written in a time before movies. The philosophical approach to life that he describes here—appreciating what is near and attending to the work at hand—is one key to Stevenson's success as a novelist.

At the beginning of a new season, especially in September,
I used to find myself, organizing, clearing out, and choosing.
Multitasking seemed to be the way to get lots of things done.
But much of the time, multitasking made me feel as if I was living in
nanoseconds, moving from one thing to another, one place to another,
different people, different tasks.
I know that part of me was energized by all the activity
and I even felt proud of all that I was accomplishing.
Now I realize that I want to focus on
one project, one person, one experience at a time.
Juggling has lost its appeal.

These reflections were made at lunch with a friend on a day when we reveled in taking time for ourselves.

Once upon a time, when I ran into friends and acquaintances,
who asked what I was up to, I would reel off a litany of activities.
Lately, I have begun to reply,
"I am practicing not multitasking."
Saying these words out loud reaffirms my intentions
and seems to give my questioners pause.

*I also pause before asking friends the reflexive "what have you been up to" question.
Instead of exchanging lists, a conversation might take place.*

Set priorities.
Focus on the most important one.

The word multitasking suggests that we can do several things simultaneously. But our brains (at least mine) can only focus on one thing at a time. My goal is to be alert to situations when too many projects have slipped into my life. When I find that I am doing too much, I try to practice not *multitasking.*

A friend alerted me to an ad for a set of tea mugs,
each inscribed with one of the following words:
creativity, tranquility, simplicity, sincerity, serenity, prosperity.

Which one would I choose? A different one each morning or always the same?

Do you want to be a woman-in-between?
Or a man-in-between?
Women (and men, too)
are looking for ways they can make time and energy for
nurturing roles and careers
that are intrinsically satisfying, rewarding financially,
and allow them to find some sort of balance.
But women and men,
individually and as couples,
must make their own trade-offs
to find balance.
Daily, weekly, monthly, and yearly.

Avant-garde women and men articulated these issues generations ago. But since the 1960s, the quest for balance is a mainstream concern in our culture. Even with the availability of high-quality day care and paid leaves for mothers and fathers after childbirth (at least for employees of large companies), it is not easy. Having worked hard to find balance when my children were growing up, I now try to support them as they (and their spouses) search for their own balance.

Living Lines

Nobody feels in control all of the time.
There is too much to do and
no one goes to bed giving thanks that he or she has
finished the day's to-do list.
When I feel overwhelmed,
I try to ask myself,
what one thing or two things
could make me feel better if done.
Often they are small chores that have been
nagging at me.

Many of us live with to-do lists. They are usually too long and have a way of increasing when we aren't paying attention. The trick is to figure out what is too long, and then stick to one's limit.

Checklist
If things are bothering me,
am I:
• exercising enough?
• doing creative things?
• sleeping enough?
• eating properly?
• doing nice things for myself?
• smiling?
• thinking of the pitcher as "half empty" rather than "half full"?
• reminding myself that I have risen to life's challenges
and will in the future?
• using my meditation tapes?
• LOVING MYSELF?

I found this checklist in a bedside table drawer when we moved from one bedroom to another during a very busy time. I knew I had written it, but did not remember how many years before. I rediscovered it at just the right moment.

Living Lines

Priorities

List the many things that you do in a day, a week, and a month.
Check the three that are the most important to you.
Are they the ones you really want to be doing?
If not, can you delegate or eliminate or re-prioritize?
Think: Essential? Desirable? Nice to do?

Most of us live with our calendars close at hand. Adding this reminder to mine at the beginning of each year helps me clarify what I do and in what order. By the way, my list is always in the process of revision.

When I feel frustrated with
what seems like my limited talents
or insufficient energy,
I have sometimes questioned God.

The answer I always get back is,
"You have what you need!"

So when I am ready to listen, I realize that I have to set priorities.
I struggle to come to terms with the fact that I can't do everything.

Now that I'm in my 60s, I face this reality frequently. It is helpful for me to remember that I felt this way when I was younger, too. I do have what I need. I just don't always recognize it.

Confusing messages on energy from my parents:
Mom: "Rest, dear; you are doing too much!"
Dad: "Don't let being tired keep you from doing something."

Decades later, I still can hear my parents' voices and their conflicting advice. Which parent to follow? With time, their differing messages have become reminders that there aren't necessarily right answers.

Anne Morrow Lindbergh, *Gift from the Sea* (New York: Pantheon Books, A Division of Random House, 1955), p. 45

The events of Anne Morrow Lindbergh's life (1906–2001) are well known. The daughter of distinguished parents, Anne was already a writer when she married transatlantic aviator and hero Charles Lindbergh at the age of 22. Marriage to an international celebrity brought press attention that was frenzied even by today's standards. Then came the shocking kidnapping of the golden couple's first child and the young family's retreat to Europe. Apparent sympathy with Germany's Fascist leaders and advocacy of nonintervention tarnished the Lindberghs' reputations, but finally allowed some measure of release from the public eye. The reflection here is from a book-length essay inspired by an island retreat that Anne made in her late 40s. Her meditations—on youth and age, love and marriage, caring for others and for one's own soul—still resonate today.

All her instinct as a woman—
the eternal nourisher of children, of men, of society—
demands that she give.
Her time, her energy, her creativeness
drain out into these channels if there is any chance, any leak.
Traditionally we are taught, and instinctively we long,
to give where it is needed—and immediately.
Eternally, woman spills herself away in driblets to the thirsty,
seldom being allowed the time, the quiet, the peace,
to let the pitcher fill up to the brim.

—Anne Morrow Lindbergh

My copy of Gift from the Sea *was given to me by my mother when I was a new mother. In this meditative book, Anne Morrow Lindbergh considers how energy can be renewed, even in the act of depletion. She offers suggestions (focus on purposeful and creative work, quiet time alone, and communion with nature), but we must all find our own methods. Have you learned how to find the balance of nurturing others and caring for yourself? Taking care of yourself is essential if you are going to nurture others. Anne Morrow Lindbergh's words are a reminder that giving and replenishing must be paired.*

SARK (aka Susan Ariel Rainbow Kennedy), *Living Juicy: Daily Morsels for Your Creative Soul* (Berkeley, California: Celestial Arts/Ten Speed Press, 1994), February 2 *(The pages of this colorful, playful book are organized by calendar dates, not conventional page numbers.)*

SARK is an author, teacher, and artist. Her efforts to inspire people to think and live more creatively have created a legion of followers. Check the *Amazon.com* review pages and you will see comments along the lines of "I absolutely adore this bizarre and wonderful book," "...very delicious to read," "You must have this book," "dangerous adventure," "neat, inspiring and weird," and many, many more along the same lines.

Who is SARK? The name Susan Ariel Rainbow Kennedy, along with the acronym SARK, came to this artist-author in two dreams. (Following the second dream, she followed through with a legal name change.) SARK's biography includes a childhood marred by trauma (though she had a vision of what she wanted to do as an adult), years of self-destructive behavior and many jobs (over 250 by the time she was in her 20s), life as a struggling (but happy) artist in San Francisco, then sudden success with a "How to Be an Artist" poster featured in an independent bookstore catalogue. Demand for the handmade poster led her to devise a production solution and become an entrepreneur. From there, it was on to her first book (*A Creative Companion*), a company and a brand (first Camp SARK, then Planet SARK), over a dozen more books, all manner of hope-inspiring products, a popular Website and even an inspirational phone line. SARK's *Daily Morsels* remains one of her most popular books, organized by weekly topics like procrastinating and avoiding perfectionism, which happen to be special issues for the author.

"The appropriate uses of Yes and No make more room for love."
Say No to what doesn't nourish you
and make a commitment to the creative in your life.

—SARK (aka Susan Ariel Rainbow Kennedy)

SARK's saucy title, "Living Juicy," is a delicious invitation to experience what more formal writers call "being fully alive." This "morsel" of advice on "completing" helps at moments when I feel a conflict between a "no" and a "yes."

Living Lines

Relationships

Two guidelines in raising children are
giving them roots and wings.
The roots I found weren't so hard,
But letting go is difficult.
We practice it in little steps as they go off
to school, to camp, to college, to someone else's hand,
…to their own lives.
The father of a 10-year-old who was at a three-week, sleep-away camp,
when asked how the family was doing said wistfully,
"She's talking about going to a sleep-away college."

We give our children life and then want to shape them into an idealized image. Think of parenting as supporting and encouraging the unfolding of a child's own gifts and talents. It will be easier to let go.

Bless the Mess!
Wishing the grandchildren lived closer and she saw them more often,
she remembered the holidays when everyone was camped
out at her house and there was a lot of noise and chaos.
Such a mess!
Now, when things are too quiet,
she and her husband laugh about the craving for the mess of the family.

By the time we have grandchildren, we know there is an ebb and flow in life. Sometimes we have too much of a good thing, and other times, too little, and we miss it. Savoring the moment, really trying to "be" with what is going on helps soften the craving during the absences.

Relationships—Children and Family

Intimacy can bring
IRRITATION.

Neatniks often pair with a messy person. The more intimate the relationship, the more space shared, the greater the potential for conflict. How can we learn to see endearing idiosyncrasies—not irritating habits—in those we love?

IRRITATION—Flipping the mirror and considering which of my habits may be irritating helps me to be more patient with my husband's sense of order. When my husband became "semi-retired" and began working at home, he took over the dishwasher detail. One afternoon, he took my still unfinished cup of tea and announced that it was time to turn on the dishwasher. Surprised, I sat for a moment and considered protesting, but I decided to make another cup of tea and be happy that he fills up the dishwasher and empties it too.

Sometimes in a relationship,
the other person doesn't have an emotional vocabulary
and needs help in understanding what we are feeling.
Make a translation from that person's own experience.

A person's emotions shift through the day. In any one day, a person may feel happy or sad, contented or angry, and various emotions in between. Shifting emotions are a fact of life. Some people can articulate what they are feeling; others act out their feelings without realizing. Keep an emotional dictionary at hand and be ready to provide translations.

Catch your behavior.
Choose what you want,
and don't pass on unresolved issues.
It can take many generations
to undo the damage of one
dysfunctional person.

I've heard "reincarnation" described as the genes and behavior that pass from one generation to the next and the next. Being conscious of what you may pass on and what old wounds you hope to heal is a lifelong awareness effort.

The accordion of generations unfolds,
incorporating genes and behaviors that have developed over
time and lifetimes.
Some work for the next generation,
but others need to be revised,
so that talents, personalities and selves
can be preserved and thrive.
Such change and preservation must be approached
with love, respect and patience.

Being human, we are reflections of our genes, our upbringing, our relationships, our social groups and our country. These inheritances don't mean that we can't adapt and change, but the process requires love, respect and patience with the generation that preceded us as much as for ourselves.

Harriet Lerner, *The Dance of Intimacy: A Woman's Guide to Courageous Acts of Change in Key Relationships* (New York: Harper & Row, Publishers, 1989), p. 189

Harriet Lerner, *The Dance of Connection: How to Talk to Someone When You're Mad, Hurt, Scared, Frustrated, Insulted, Betrayed, or Desperate* (New York: HarperCollins Publishers, 2001), p. 26

A native Brooklynite, Harriet Goldhor Lerner, Ph.D., has practiced psychotherapy in Kansas since the 1970s. Well-known for her work on the psychology of women and family relationships, she is a best-selling author, skilled at translating theoretical writing on family systems for a general audience. In addition to her nine books on relationships (one based on her advice column), she is the author (with her sister, Susan Goldhor) of two children's books.

Dr. Lerner's books reassure us that we—and our relationships—are works in process. Further, though we can only change ourselves, change must be made in step with others —parents, partners and children. As Meryl Streep says in the movie, "It's complicated…," but Harriet Lerner's books offer good practical advice to bring to the dance.

The degree to which we can be clear with our first family about
who we are, what we believe, and where we stand on important issues
will strongly influence the level of "independence" or
emotional maturity
that we bring to other relationships.

—Harriet Lerner

…[the] perfect family doesn't exist.
In my many years of clinical practice,
I haven't met the family that even begins to fit this description….
I do know that the family is a sensitive system,
reacting to the predictable stresses of the life cycle…
and to unanticipated stresses…
many painful things
have happened in the history of a family long before we enter the scene,
and when issues are unresolved in one generation,
they are often reenacted in the next.

—Harriet Lerner

Relationships—Children and Family

Sydney Callahan is a psychologist, mother of six and author of *Parents Forever: You and Your Adult Children*. She has written articles, books, and columns (and now blogs) for *America* magazine on religious, psychological and ethical questions. She was one of the first psychologists to write about the problems faced by working mothers, and more recently, about the long years of shifting relations between parents and adult children.

No one told you
this job of raising adult children
would go on so long.

—An observation made by my friend, Sydney Callahan

We might sometimes ask, who is raising whom? The relationship between a parent and child continues for decades after the child leaves home and even after one departs this earth.

A close family friend, married to a bishop,
was often asked about her marriage.
Questioners assumed that theirs was an easy relationship.
She startled the questioners by replying that,
at least once a day, she wanted to kill her husband
and thought that their marriage had no hope for survival.
They were married for 50 years.

This lovely woman probably helped as many people with her honesty as did her husband with his sermons. Making the effort even when the feeling of love seems remote is what makes a relationship. I heard long ago, love is not a feeling, but a decision.

Everywhere she went,
she brought flowers.

—A gravestone inscription written by a husband
in memory of his wife, who died very young,
as cited in Robert J. Wicks, *Riding the Dragon*, p. 38

Dr. James A. Coan, a psychologist at the University of Virginia, as quoted in an article on the results of a neuroscience research study of the effect of human touch on neural response to threatening situations. Benedict Carey, "Holding Loved One's Hand Can Calm Jittery Neurons," *New York Times,* January 31, 2006, p. D7

Holding Loved One's Hand Can Calm Jittery Neurons

The effect of this simple gesture of social support
is that the brain and the body don't have to work as hard,
they're less stressed in response to a threat.

—Dr. James A. Coan

It's gratifying when researchers confirm something that we know instinctively!

Frederick Buechner, *Secrets in the Dark: A Life in Sermons* (New York: HarperCollins Publishers, 2006), p. 183

American writer and theologian, Frederick Buechner (1926–), had already written a critically acclaimed novel, *A Long Day's Dying*, when he was drawn into an intense search for understanding of his own inner faith. Still in his 20s at the time, he was inspired to go to Union Theological Seminary, where he studied with Reinhold Niebuhr and Paul Tillich. An ordained Presbyterian minister, Reverend Buechner has combined his calling as a minister and writer. Through his words— written and spoken—he makes the case for faith in God.

Reverend Buechner has been much quoted in Sunday sermons and elsewhere, including by John Irving, his former student at Exeter, in the preface to *A Prayer for Owen Meany*. The reflection that I have included here is cited with particular frequency. It is drawn not from a sermon, but from a talk given at the New York Public Library entitled "Faith and Fiction." As a theologian and fiction writer, Reverend Buechner makes the case that seeming contradictions may have fundamental elements in common.

I first found this reflection by Frederick Buechner in another minister's sermon. Once aware of it, I recognized Reverend Buechner's words in many other places. On reading the full talk, I find them even more affecting. To quote another reflection in his essay, "Faith and Fiction," "A coincidence can be, as somebody has said, God's way of remaining anonymous, or it can be just a coincidence…Whether we bet Yes or No, it is equally an act of faith." (p. 172)

Living Lines

People come and go.
The scene shifts.
Time runs by, runs out.
Maybe it is all utterly meaningless.
Maybe it is all unutterably meaningful.
If you want to know which, pay attention....
The unexpected sound of your name on somebody's lips.
The good dream.
The odd coincidence...
Maybe even the smallest events hold the greatest clues...
Pay attention.
As a summation of all that I have had to say as a writer,
I would settle for that.
And as a talisman or motto for that journey in search of a homeland,
which is what faith is,
I would settle for that too.

—Frederick Buechner

Anaïs Nin (1903–1977) is known for many reasons—her erotic writing, her bohemian lifestyle, her complicated relationships, and exotic parentage with French, Cuban, and Danish roots, but most of all for her diaries. Begun when she was 11 years old, Nin's diaries span more than six decades and document an extraordinary life of friendships.

Each friend represents a world in us,
a world possibly not born until he or she arrives.

—Anaïs Nin, with thanks to my friend Susan.

I have a bouquet of friends, each one different. I find myself revealing—sometimes discovering—different aspects of myself with each of them.

A friend needs
the song in your heart
and can sing it back to you
when you need it.

In some ways, friends are mirrors to us, and at times, we can be mirrors to them.
Friends can know how to sing words of encouragement and love—music to our hearts—
when we need them. I think that one of the signs of real friendship is a reciprocity of
keeping in touch.

There are times when feelings seem to be
just at the edge of our awareness.

A sudden uneasy sensation. A fluttering of the heart. Signals of feelings waiting to be expressed? Sometimes, such sensations are just mysterious, passing perceptions. Other times, I realize that a fluttering is a signal of a feeling waiting to be acknowledged. Occasionally, I recognize that I have received a message, but only in retrospect.

A kind heart sometimes
breaks the protectiveness
I have built around the pain.

I am grateful when
compassion gives me permission
to acknowledge the burdens,
even cry a little.

A stiff upper lip—attempting to control our emotions by not showing them—may not be the best way to cope.

Thoughtful is someone
whose kindly thoughts
are translated into action.

Having moved over a dozen times, I have been fortunate to make many more friends than I might have otherwise. These friends have shown thoughtfulness in many ways, small and large, and I try to do the same. Over time, acts of kindness have deepened our connections, despite geographical separation. Occasionally, after I have been thinking of a particular friend, she will call and say, "I've been thinking of you." Or vice versa.

If only we had known…

How many times have we all said to ourselves, "If only I had know, I would have…" The "would have" might have been a call or visit or just understanding some uncharacteristic behavior. It is so easy to live as if there will always be tomorrows, but hard, too, because doing so will lead to regrets of what might have been.

Wanting to show my concern,
I used to ask about a someone's illness or express sympathy at a loss
until I realized that
it may be the one moment in the day
when he or she is distracted from the pain.
So I try to let that person know
I am thinking of him or her without asking.

There is a fine line between being solicitous and not referring to the illness or loss. Often a friend is relieved not to talk about pain directly, but just as often some topic breaks through and eyes tear. Being together in that moment can mean more than words.

Sharing our mutual wisdom
has always been a gift of our friendship.
Sometimes I think I have
found mine in our conversations.

This reflection is dedicated to a dear friend. Some writers say that they write to discover what they think as they weigh words and viewpoints before committing them to paper. I feel this way about conversations with my friend. Our friendship has given me the possibility of creative "thinking out loud" as I weigh my contributions during our wonderful talks. I hope that my friend feels this way about me.

One benefit of a difficult time is recognizing our own vulnerability and then being able to meet other people in theirs.

My relationships with family and friends have deepened when we have shared our vulnerabilities—euphemistically called our "human side." Though our culture often encourages strength in the face of adversity, it is really the sharing of our woundedness than binds us to one another and to God.

We often judge others' outsides from our own inside,
or we judge our own insides by others' outsides.
We look at others as calm,
in control,
on top of things.
For many people,
it takes a lot of effort
to put themselves together and
what you see is
the result of that effort,
not the challenge of getting there.

I am startled when someone tells me that I always seem "so calm," especially at moments when I have lots of emotions going on inside. As I grow older, I have been more willing to reveal some of those inner feelings. The result can be closer relationships.

During a serious illness,
you need to realize
how little most things matter,
and learn to let people help.

A serious illness or accident will quickly make a patient and his or her family focus on what they really need. What can be hard is accepting that the help of friends can be part of what they need. Given my own impulse to be private and self-sufficient, I try to hold this truth in mind.

Sharon Gersten Luckman, as told to Juston Jones, "OFFICE SPACE: THE BOSS; Back-Office Choreographer," *The New York Times,* January 29, 2006

Sharon Gersten Luckman has been Executive Director of Alvin Ailey American Dance Theater since 1995. A dancer in school and college, Sharon Luckman has played a major off-stage role in the expansion of the Alvin Ailey Dance Foundation for nearly 20 years.

Judith Jamison—widely considered Alvin Ailey's greatest dancer—became Artistic Director of the company in 1989 following Ailey's untimely death. Recipient of numerous awards including the National Medal for the Arts, Ms. Jamison was actually "discovered" by Agnes de Mille (quoted on page 25).

Sign on the door of the Executive Director of the
Alvin Ailey American Dance Theater:

"I don't have the answer.
I like to work with people
who like solving things together."

—Sharon Gersten Luckman

Alvin Ailey directors, Judith Jamison and Sharon Luckman, are quite a team. In planning the Alvin Ailey's golden anniversary year, they sought to bring dance to every-one, which they did by organizing street dances, free performances and classes, as well as a 50-city tour. Their goals—move spirits and lift people right off the ground. Having attended one of those 50th anniversary performances, I can say that they accomplished the goal of levitating the audience; by the end of the performance, my husband and I felt as if we were floating!

As the title of John Gray's book says,
"Men are from Mars,
Women are from Venus."
Men want to solve problems.
Women want to be heard, share emotions.
Listening might be the answer for both.

The best lesson from John Gray's popular book comes down to this basic truth: Listen and truly hear what you are saying and what the other person says in response. I have read that studies on communication indicate as little as seven percent of what we say is understood in the way we intended. (It is a wonder that we understand each other at all!) My rule of thumb is to listen for the meaning of my own words.

Coping

Alice (Ali) Domar has been pioneering the application of mind/body medicine to women's health since earning her Ph.D. in health psychology from the Albert Einstein College of Medicine's joint program with Yeshiva University. As a faculty member at the Harvard Medical School, Dr. Domar has pursued two research goals: understanding the relation between stress and women's health and developing programs to help women alleviate the physical and psychological symptioms of stress. At the same time, she has been a leader in translating the latest medical research to a wider audience in a series of best-selling books. With the support of Boston IVF, Dr. Domar founded the first mind/body center for women's health.

What is new and good today?

—Ali Domar's "patented" personal greeting

Many of us "unload" our problems on those closest to us
when we walk in the door at the end of the day.
A better way to reenter each other's presence is to share
what is new and good today!

Working with Ali to develop a corporate stress reduction program for the Mind/Body Institute, I learned the power of these positive words. If only "What is new and good today?" signs flashed when we got home at the end of the day. Ali Domar's question reminds me to greet my family and friends with the good news.

A series of small responsibilities can accumulate into
a burden that is too much.

How often do you hear someone say—"Oh, I'll take care of myself after THIS is all over"? And then the next thing occurs and the next. Even small things, when multiplied, become large. At some point, exhaustion takes over.

Be relieved that there is something that can be done about it.

—My father

When there is a problem, health issue or another difficult challenge,
be grateful for the availability of remedies,
even if they are not magic cures.

When a thorny issue came up in our family, I remember my father, a doctor, consoling us by saying that at least there were remedies available. So often I have thought of this way of looking at problems, remembering that many problems can be solved or at least alleviated.

General George C. Marshall, as quoted in "The Truman Memoirs: Part II," *Life Magazine,* January 30, 1956, p. 76

The first American general to receive five-star rank, General George Marshall (1880–1959) was Chief of Staff of the U.S. Army during World War II with responsibility for overseeing the largest military build-up in the country's history. Following the war, General Marshall served as Secretary of State and then Secretary of Defense. A testament to his greatness as an administrator is the unreserved praise of Franklin Roosevelt, Harry Truman and Winston Churchill. In 1953, he was awarded the Nobel Peace Prize for his plan to rebuild postwar Europe, better known as the Marshall Plan.

General Marshall reportedly made the comment on the facing page as Secretary of State, at a department staff meeting where the debate was more extended than the general was used to. Another well-known Marshall aphorism is: "Military power wins battles, but spiritual power wins wars."

Gentlemen, don't fight the problem;
decide it.

—General George C. Marshall

With all due respect to General Marshall, before "deciding" problems, I ask: Is it really a problem? Is it my problem?

Arthur Wellesley, Duke of Wellington, as quoted in Sir Herbert Maxwell, *The Life of Wellington: The Restoration of the Martial Power of Great Britain* (London: Sampson, Low, Martin and Company, 1899), p. 67

The First Duke of Wellington (1769–1852) famed for his leadership in defeating Napoleon I at Waterloo, was also known as a tireless worker. The words here, recorded by the Earl of Stanhope, were Wellington's response to a questioner, who expressed astonishment that the great military leader was able to write so much in the midst of active operations.

My rule has always been to do the business of the day in the day.

—Arthur Wellesley, Duke of Wellington

William Osler, *A Way of Life* (Baltimore: The Remington-Putnam Book company, 1932), p. 17 (emphasis in the original)

Sir William Osler (1849–1919) was a Canadian physician, variously called the father of modern medicine (for introducing a clinical component into the medical school curriculum) or the father of "psychosomatic medicine" (for recognizing the importance of a patient's state of mind). Though Sir Osler's career was one of great distinction, he did not forget the anxiety he felt as a young medical student, overwhelmed at the amount of knowledge to be absorbed, with lingering doubts about the past and concern for the unknown future. Osler's famous advice was imparted to a graduating class at Johns Hopkins School of Medicine, and later given wide circulation—with credit—by Dale Carnegie.

Now the way of life that I preach
is a habit to be acquired gradually by long and steady repetition.
It is the practice of living for the day only, and for the day's work,
Live in day-tight compartments.

—William Osler

Can we live in the moment, in the day, not in the past or focused on the future? I try to practice asking myself, "Where is my mind now—past, present or future?"

James Keenan, S.J., Personal note

James Keenan, S.J. is a professor of theological ethics at Boston College. Father Keenan's approach is direct and personal, he considers the big traditional virtues—charity, justice, temperance, courage, but also the smaller ones—fidelity, self-esteem, hospitality, gratitude and truthfulness. He draws his readers to the central question, "Who should I be?"

The grace of self-doubt
keeps us from holding on to certitudes
that are not that certain.

—James Keenan, S.J.

I met Father Keenan some years ago at St. Peter, a Catholic church that is a short walk from my house. He regularly said the 5 o'clock Mass and often spoke at a church lecture series. I soon learned why those 5 o'clock Masses and lectures were so well attended! Father Keenan sees virtues not as "ideas," but as "practices," and therefore, views the forming a conscience as a lifelong process. He focuses, not on sin and punishment, but on how to be the best person one can be.

Robert P. Wicks, *Riding the Dragon: Ten Lessons for Inner Strength in Challenging Times* (Notre Dame, Indiana: Sorin Books, 2003), pp. 91–92

In giving the advice here, Professor Wicks offers a gardening metaphor based on experience planting new annuals for his mother. Task accomplished, so he thought, his mother observed that he was just scratching on the surface and instructed him to "dig down deep and shake up the soil…[so that the fertilizer can] mix down deep in the soil where it's needed." When he expressed fear about "rough treatment" of the roots of the new plants, his mother reassured, "Shaking up can be very good for growth."

Even when it hurts,
we need to seek as much clarity about our lives as possible…
Pain can be a transition to new life if it isn't avoided or feared.

—Robert P. Wicks

Freud described the pleasure/pain cycle. We are drawn to pleasure and resist pain. In resisting, the pain can become more intense. Knowing this, I ask, "What is the pain teaching me?" Can I embrace fear, acknowledge it and so reduce it?

When I feel overwhelmed,
I ask myself,
What one or two things can I do to alleviate the anxiety?
Often those things are small, mundane tasks,
that can be done quickly,
relieving the pressure and making it easier to move on to other things.

This approach has helped me many times, whether moving to a new city or the routine demands of daily life. One summer long ago, I kept thinking about all the endless family ironing. My solution: I put an ironing board and iron in a convenient closet, and ironed clothes as needed each day, not more, not less.

Living Lines

The last year has been a coil.
As the coil unwinds,
I feel the coil's tension and anxiety
diffuse with the gradual unwinding.

Imagine a large rubber band that has been tightly twisted. As you begin to unwind it, there continues to be tension. Sometimes, I don't realize how much tension I have been experiencing until I start to release some of the pressure.

Sue Monk Kidd, *When the Heart Waits: Spiritual Direction for Life's Sacred Questions* (New York, Harper and Row, 1990), p. 114

Sue Monk Kidd (1948–) published her first novel, the phenomenally successful, *The Secret Life of Bees,* when she was in her mid-50s. Trained as a nurse, she worked in nursing for a decade before shifting to writing. Though her goal was to write fiction, she took a longer path through nonfiction, notably as a successful freelancer for *Guideposts* magazine. Her book, *When the Heart Waits,* is a milestone along the way. Written just after her 40th birthday, it is a story of midlife spiritual crisis, of painful stirrings, of inner voices seeking expression. Did she dare "disturb the universe" within herself? During the solitude of a winter's walk, Ms. Kidd happened upon a cocoon hanging from a dogwood branch, and recognized the fragile structure as a symbol of a new true self, waiting to be born. In describing the next months and into a new year, she shows that the "crucible of transformation" is in the waiting.

Letting go is like releasing a tight spring at the core of yourself,
one you've spent your whole life winding and maintaining.
When you let go,
you grow still and silent.

—Sue Monk Kidd

The words "still and silent" are paired and repeated in many books on spirituality.

I feel like I have crossed through wild winds
into the calm eye of the storm.
I must face the wildness again
because the calm will pass.

I am learning to be aware of not "attaching" to a particular state of mind, pleasurable or painful. Each state will inevitably change. Be engaged, conscious of what is happening, but do not try to hold onto one particular time.

Living Lines

Fake it
'til you
make it.

For me, this popular advice doesn't mean being phony. It makes me approach challenging situations as dress rehearsals. Eventually, I'll be ready for a performance. Imagining what I want to be or do helps me take steps in the direction of my concert debut.

Robert J. Wicks, *Riding the Dragon* (Notre Dame, Indiana: Sorin Books, 2003), pp. 70–71

The lines here come from a chapter entitled "Seek Hidden Possibilities." Professor Wicks makes the case that "avoiding unnecessary worrying is essential so we can both live fully and be there for others."

The distinction between worry and concern has been very helpful and insightful for me. Becoming aware that I am worrying helps me use my energy in a healthier way. Learning to "sit" with a trouble gives me time to develop a perspective on what I can do and sometimes that means accepting the problem and not trying to "fix" it.

Living Lines

Worry is debilitating because it glues us to the problem.
Concern, on the other hand, is freeing because it lets us sit along
the issues, fears, sadness, losses,
and uncontrollable and undesirable events
that come our way.
But letting go of worry is not so straightforward.
Otherwise, so many people wouldn't worry so much...
"How can I sit with this trouble in a good way?"
Worry encourages us to spend all our energy wringing our hands over
something. Concern looks at how we can show mercy toward
the issue or person involved and thus respond with compassion.
This attitude of mercy, coupled with a spirit of humility,
is at the heart of true concern.
It helps us to determine, given our own limits,
what we can do about something.

—Robert J. Wicks

Pain is the resistance to what is.

Tightening up around a physical or emotional pain makes it worse. Breathing into it allows some release.

Many of the things we complain about are
problems of the privileged.
Privilege can mean many things.
Thinking of things that way
can keep our complaints and problems
in perspective.

*We've lived for much of the last decade in a culture that changed what were once
considered luxuries into necessities. I know that I am privileged in so many ways, but
most especially in the love of my family and friends.*

Often our drug of choice is our own adrenaline
and we can become addicted to it.
This is one reason that meditation and quiet time are so important.
Sometimes we don't even realize we are on a drug
because it is self-manufactured.

The pace of life in this multitasking, 24/7 world seems to require a steady dose of adrenaline. It is easy to ignore how much we can depend on that rush. Meditation, quiet time, and prayer can slow us down. Breathing with awareness can help us to fill our bodies with oxygen, not adrenaline.

Once or twice a day, it is helpful to lie down on the floor,
stretching with awareness
and paying attention to the places that are tight,
need some extra oxygen.
Breathe into those areas to release the tension.
When you stop and pay attention this way,
you will find that your body feels different each time.
Therefore, each time that you stretch, ask yourself,
am I centered in my body now?

When I let too much time go between following this advice, my awareness of my body changes, sometimes very much so. The contrast reminds me to be more diligent in my practice of stretching, breathing, and centering.

Every day it's the same old thing:
Breathe, breathe, breathe.
What a wondrous thing breathing is!

Take a mini-vacation—in a warm relaxing shower or bath, waiting for the computer to boot up, standing in a grocery line or at a long red light, the days are full of possibilities. These are moments to breathe.

On the days when your insides
don't seem together,
put special effort into your outsides.
It's called
putting yourself together from the outside in.

Remembering "outside in" helps when I am upset or tired. Over time, I think this from-the-outside approach can build a stronger center. Sometimes, I ask myself, "Is the 'reality' what others see or what I feel inside?"

Years ago, I went to a career-planning course.
In one exercise, we were told to place ourselves in a line
where we thought we belonged in the group.
I placed myself fourth or fifth.
Everyone seemed to have a clear idea of where
he or she felt comfortable.
We were then told to rearrange the line as to how we thought each
person fit.
Everyone placed me at the front of the line.
I remember it so clearly because
my comfort level is more behind the scenes.
When I'm asked to lead,
I think of that course.

Although I took that course 30 years ago, I still remember it and reflect on where my comfort level is. Growth is possible when we step out of our comfort zone.

I am growing
more comfortable
with my uncomfortableness.

I wrote this line many years ago. As I read it with fresh eyes, I realize that most growth comes from dealing with discomfort.

A smile changes
body chemistry.

Try lying in bed.
Think of the good things in your day.

Smile.

I try this exercise, even when I am not going to sleep. It makes me feel happier, lifting my spirits. It is often said that smiling changes one's emotional chemistry. In my experience, it does.

"So be perfect as your heavenly Father is perfect"
is a hard standard to live up to.
As I grow older, I embrace the humanity of God
as a more realistic goal.
It doesn't pay to be a perfectionist.
That doesn't mean striving for imperfection.

I internalized the "So be perfect..." line from the New Testament (Matt. 5:48) as a girl. Now I struggle to accept myself as I am and not to worry that I don't measure up to an unrealistic ideal.

After decades of trying to be perfect, to make things perfect,
GOOD ENOUGH
is more comfortable and more realistic.
It makes me more patient with myself
and with others, too.

Perfection is an impossible goal. GOOD ENOUGH isn't settling. I am still learning that.

Trust the Mess (Coping Version)

Often in the midst of a difficult situation,
I find that life is just plain messy,
no matter how much effort or organization is devoted to the matter.
Over time,
I have learned that
trusting is the best attitude.
Trust the mess
and trust that, with time,
your efforts
will contribute to a resolution.

As I learn to "trust the mess," I find that organizational effort is important, but sometimes so is "letting go." Continuous attempts to organize out of a situation may be too controlling and even stand in the way of a solution.

When you move or change your frame of reference,
you can't be on Automatic Pilot.
After one move,
I couldn't remember my street number when I applied
for a supermarket card.
Feeling stupid,
I recovered enough to remember that the
four-digit number was painted on the curb.
I asked my four-year-old son what the number on the curb was and
he told me "4215."
Saved by "Sesame Street" learning!

We moved 12 times in our first 27 years of marriage. After the last move, I noticed that I could work on the larger projects before turning to the smaller ones. But sometimes, the process is reversed; working on the details builds to the big picture.

I prepare for my return
as much as my departure.

For 10 years, I traveled with my husband on his business trips to destinations around the globe. Adding up 10 years of intense travel—one week here, 10 days there, occasionally three-weeks, two (sometimes three) trips per month (with time off for good behavior in August and December)—makes my head spin. The shortest trips were within the United States. More than 30 were to European cities, and 20-plus were to Australia, Hong Kong, Singapore, Japan, China and Vietnam.

I quickly learned to become really organized for our departures, and almost as quickly, that it was just as important to plan well for the return home. Early during this time of fast-paced traveling, I noticed that my husband seemed to unpack much faster than I did. His secret? He sent everything to the drycleaners! I began to follow his lead, and from then on, I was unpacked just as quickly.

Coping

When you feel life is too intense,
imagine it as a TV soap opera.
Turn the sound down until it seems manageable
or mute the sound and read the text.
It reads differently than it sounds.

This idea came to mind when I was sitting in a high-tech dentist chair and there was a soap opera on the TV screen. The sound was turned off and the script appeared in captions. The goings-on seemed less dramatic that way. Sometimes we can't eliminate the drama in our lives, but we can turn the volume down.

Why do we have the illusion that life should be easy?

Until we can embrace the hard times, the losses,
we will always be surprised
when illness, pain, loss and disappointment come into our lives.
Sometimes all at the same time.

Reciting "The Welcoming Prayer" in Reverend Cynthia Bourgeault's book, Centering Prayer and Inner Awakening, *is a very helpful way to "be" with the difficult things in life, even a painful thought or feeling. The "welcoming" brings on "awareness," giving the experience space to clarify its meaning.*

Sometimes it is good to
make plans for your day.
Sometimes it is good to
let the day be what is.

I look at my calendar to see if there is enough open time for me to just be. I like to let some part of my day unfold without planning. And on days when this luxury isn't possible, I try to add at least a bit of extra exercise or quiet time.

As members of the "Greatest Generation"
reach the end of their lives,
it surprises me that many of them
have spoken of their experiences and their pain only then.

As the wife of a two-tour Vietnam veteran,
I assumed it was only
that unpopular war's stories and pain that were suppressed.

We are living through wars in Afghanistan and Iraq,
and in the aftermath of 9/11,
our shores no longer feel as safe as they once did.
Will the horrors and pain of the past decade be suppressed, too?

Members of the press, embedded with the troops, have reported the Iraq and Afghanistan Wars in graphic detail. Computers and cell phones connect soldiers and their families. Will extensive reporting and real-time connections allow members of this generation to heal sooner than their fathers and grandfathers?

We often criticize ourselves for
not making a decision.
But very often, we don't act
because we don't have enough information
or it is not the right time.
It can be a combination of both.
When you are feeling stuck
or in limbo,
look back
and ask if you can remember
being in this kind of situation before.

I try to remind myself not to be critical of decisions that I haven't made.

Do you sometimes feel Sick Tired?

One often hears the phrase, "sick and tired."
Sick Tired is a step beyond.
It you are Sick Tired, it is a time to pay special attention to yourself.

My sisters and I find this word pairing helpful. When it comes to mind, we pay attention and think about slowing down. Recognizing that we are Sick Tired can be a blessing— a reminder to care for ourselves and each other.

Coping

When I am tired and perhaps achy,
it is difficult not to react with frustration.
Who wants to be tired?
But I am learning that feeling tired or achy is often a protective gift,
courtesy of body, mind, and spirit.

The body's reactions to physical and mental activity are protective messages and should be welcomed. I am learning to listen more carefully to my body's wisdom.

When I asked a lovely older couple, who still lead a very busy life,
how they manage it all,
they both smiled and replied,
"Sometimes you hide out and you don't tell."

I have shared their secret, which is now also mine, with many people. The hiding out can be a day, an evening, 10 minutes. However short, take some time for yourselves. "Hide out and don't tell" can be your secret, too.

The Ursuline Order was founded in 1535 by St. Angela Merici (1474–1540), primarily for the education of girls and the sick and the needy. Orphaned at the age of 10, the young Angela dedicated herself to God, but that dedication did not stifle her pilgrim's courage or prevent her from leading a life in the world. In this spirit, she founded an order that offered women an alternative to marriage or the convent.

Do something, get moving, be confident, risk new things, stick with it...
and be ready for big surprises.

—Newsletter from my high school, the Ursuline School in New Rochelle, New York.

I keep these lines—which translate the centuries-old Ursuline precept into modern terms—on a card hanging over my desk. Many mornings, I read these words and find the encouragement to do something, even something small. They propel me out of the starting gate.

Judge Joan Lefkow as quoted by Mary Schmich, "The Journey of Judge Joan Lefkow," *Chicago Tribune,* November 20, 2005

Judge Lefkow's husband and mother were murdered by the plaintiff in a medical malpractice suit that she had dismissed. Judge Lefkow had to accept their loss, and also the knowledge that it was she who had been the killer's intended target, not her husband or mother, who were both in the house by chance on that fateful day.

There is no court of appeal that can reverse what has happened.
We have to live with it and in spite of it
I pray that one day joy will return to our lives,
and I believe that will happen.

—Judge Joan Lefkow

Each day, the news brings stories of other people's hardships and tragedies to our attention. Judge Lefkow received an enormous outpouring of sympathy; others suffer with much less notice. In either case, the bereaved one must accept that there is no fixing or repairing what has been broken, and then summon the courage to go on with life, even to find happiness again.

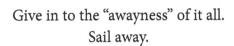

Give in to the "awayness" of it all.
Sail away.

Whether you have only a few moments or a long-planned vacation, we all need a certain amount of "awayness"—disconnecting, releasing, relaxing, just being.

Be in the moment.
Play.
Rest.
Nap.
Pat yourself on the back.
Smile.

Pruning

Clear away what
you don't need,
and what
you don't really want,
but have gotten used to.

I have been in a clearing-out mode for the last few months—books, clothes, flowerpots tucked away after the plants died. For the first 25 years of our marriage, we used to move every three years or so, and it was easier to de-accession possessions we no longer used. But we've lived in our present home for nearly two decades, so I have to look hard at things to see if they still belong here. When we cleared out several hundred books from our shelves and brought them to the book trailer at the town dump, the supervisor asked my husband what he thought of the empty shelves. He answered, "She loves them."

Living Lines

When asked how good a golfer, painter, writer…I am,
I sometimes answer,
I like to do a lot of different things;
If I judged how well I did each of them,
I might not have so much fun trying!
I am learning, trying, to be comfortable with that answer.

New York Mayor Koch was once known for asking, "How'm I doin'?" Sometimes, it seems that when you take up an activity—golf, tennis, yoga—people expect that you will strive to become an expert. Of course, it's nice to be known for doing something well. But the more I relax, the more I enjoy my various pursuits, the less I worry about how well I'm doing.

My get up and go
got up and went!

In our fast-paced lives, can we admit that we need more down time and more rest? That we can't bounce out of bed each morning? I try to, and I've learned that pacing myself— respecting my own peaks and valleys—allows me to make the most of the energy I have.

Sometimes it is hard
to stop
wanting to skip ahead,
and accept the need to stay
in place now.

When I was a little girl, going to confession weekly, I remember invariably repeating penitently—10 times, "Bless me, Father, for I have been impatient." As an adult, I could say the same, but 10 x 10. Patience is being accepting of the moment, and the next, and the next, and so on.

Henri Nouwen as quoted by Robert J. Wicks, *Riding the Dragon: Ten Lessons for Inner Strength in Challenging Times* (Notre Dame, Indiana: Sorin Books, 2003), p. 33.

Henri Nouwen (1932–1996) was a Dutch Catholic priest, whose writings on spirituality emphasize that we are the beloved sons and daughters of God. Robert Wicks began to integrate religion into his work as a young psychologist. In his recent book, he tells of visiting Henri Nouwen to seek the older man's counsel on work and life, and especially on the topic of "availability." Nouwen noted that availability was a gift, but one that came with dangers, and then offered the advice quoted here.

Pruning…
not only speaks of cutting back
but also of the ultimate blossoming
that takes place when it is done properly.

—Henri Nouwen

In horticulture, pruning encourages growth. But knowing where to cut to maximize that growth requires some expertise. The image of pruning has become increasingly important to me. One place where I've tried to prune is my natural impulse to solve someone else's problems rather than support that person's own decisions.

Think of taking a "sabbatical"
from the routines in your life
that don't seem to be working.
You may decide,
with some perspective,
to modify your usual patterns or even to drop them.
Evaluate the activities that are meaningful to you.
Who wants to be carrying baggage,
that was once important, but no longer is?
Travel lighter.

Creating more space and time for myself is a priority for me now. I can't do everything that I once did, and I don't want to either.

In a time of transition,
don't fill the space and time
until you experience it.

Our fear in transitions is that there will be a vacuum. Too often, we react by trying to fill our calendars with new projects. Resist this urge.

Jon Kabat-Zinn, *Wherever You Go There You Are: Mindfulness Meditation in Everyday Life* (New York: Hyperion, 1994), pp. 192–193

Jon Kabat-Zinn notes that, in the stress-reduction clinic, others tend to look to him as the authority—as the person who will tell them how to relax, to get their lives together, to discover the key to mindfulness. Rather than play the authority role, he encourages patients to become their own authorities.

Recently, when we were riding our bikes on a new route, my husband said that it would be fine to ride on the sidewalk, even though a telephone pole was looming right in the middle. I decided to make my own decision and walked past the pole. A small incident, but an example of listening to my own feelings.

Living Lines

What is required to participate more fully
in our own health and well-being
is simply to listen more carefully
and to trust what we hear,
to trust the messages from our own life,
from our own body and mind and feelings...
Developing such an attitude means authoring one's own life
and, therefore, assuming some measure of authority oneself.
It requires believing in oneself.

—Jon Kabat-Zinn

Say as in RAP,
When you're on the fast track,
nobody gives you any slack.

The fast pace of a life with 24/7 demands can leave very little breathing room for just being or flexibility for unexpected events. When I was in college, I spent one summer working at a law firm in New York City. Lunch was an hour's time to eat and shop. I often noticed that even though I didn't have to hurry, I was walking quickly to keep the pace with the others on the sidewalk. That was decades ago, but the pace of life is like that sidewalk speedwalking. I am aware that it is better to choose my own pace.

I ran out of gas.

—So said my much older next-door neighbor to explain
why she went to bed for a week after the holidays.

In our caffeinated society, the message is caffeine and sugar will help put you in motion—make it possible to get along with less sleep. Admitting to myself (and to others) that I need to restore my energy—to fill up my tank—is an adjustment. Learning to say "not now" is okay.

Go Slow
So you can Go Fast.
Take the time to build a strong foundation.
Be Patient.

At one time, my tendency was to equate efficiency with speed. Experience has taught me that it is often better to go slowly, to build a firm foundation.

Taking Care of Yourself

Buy things you need and want;
don't go to the sale rack and buy what is left over.
(Of course, if what you want and need is on sale, it's your lucky day!)

Many of us learned to give ourselves what was left over after we attended to others'
needs. At least occasionally, put yourself first.

We often have an abundance of the real things in life.

If only I had "this," "that" would happen. "Then, I would be happy." When I catch these if-then thoughts, I remind myself, "Stop and appreciate the wonderful people and experiences in your life now."

If you want to gain insight and build trust,
look around 360 degrees.

Is there ever a time when we can see 360 degrees? Wisdom comes from looking for our center and then gently turning around so that we may see from the perspective of those looking at us.

Hillel the Elder was a Jewish sage and scholar of the Torah, one of the greatest of rabbis, who was active in Jerusalem from 30 B.C.E to 10 C.E. Known for his humble and patient character as well as his brevity, the reflection on the facing page is one of his most famous. Rabbi Hillel's other much-quoted adage is, "What is hateful to you, don't do to your fellow man—that's the whole Torah, and the rest…is just commentary."

If I am not for myself,
who will be for me?
If I am only for myself,
what am I?
And if not now,
when?

—Rabbi Hillel the Elder

As a girl, I felt that my life was to be focused on helping others, and it seemed that there was always more to give. With time and hard-won experience, I learned that I must also nurture myself. If I give myself what I need, there will be more to give others. If I don't, my well runs dry. And with a dry well, it may be difficult to take advantage of those moments when, as Hillel suggests, action should be taken.

Pruning

Sometimes you don't know how much
you are carrying until you put
down the load and
feel it in all of
your body, mind and spirit.

For years, I responded to the challenges in my life, thinking I was aware of how much I was carrying. But there came a time when my body told me I needed to put down my load for a while. The process of letting go of the accumulated weight helped me see that things weighed more than I had realized.

I'm not old.
I've just lived a long time.

—Anonymous

Demographers have defined new age categories out of the broad groupings of "middle age" and "old age." Where there were once two categories, now there are many—"nearly middle age," "younger middle age," "middle age," "older middle age," "young old age," et cetera. It's a sliding scale. Where do wisdom and experience begin to fit into the picture?

As we grow older,
we have to learn to
honor our limits.

This advice can be more challenging than it seems. Here are two questions to help:
"Is there a limit to what I can do?" or, in the spirit of "been there, done that," is it really,
"Is it time to pass some of my longtime assignments to others?"

As we grow older,
we need to help each other.
She has arthritis and needs help putting on her jewelry.
He needs his glasses.
Together, they put on her necklace.

We fear our vulnerability, especially as our birthdays bring us closer to old age. The need to ask for help may seem like surrender, but surrendering expands the intimacy that could be better used for another purpose.

When is life or
our response to it,
just enough
or too much?

When life is demanding,
can we build in some flexibility?

What if our lives are
right on the edge,
and we don't see
the precipice?

The answer lies in discernment.

We all need to learn to
set limits.

Do you live in an
unnaturally high setting for normal?

Are you expecting
too much of
yourself and others?

Remember to ask yourself these questions. It's easy to begin driving over the speed limit without realizing it.

Do the best you can
with what you have.
Enjoy the ride.

—The secret of one 90-year-old

If we aren't satisfied doing our best with what we have, we won't enjoy what we did accomplish.

How easy it is to get something done
when no one is trying to take credit for it.

It is very human to expect credit or praise for what we do. But the dynamic of the doing is different when we aren't looking over our shoulder to see if someone is observing our good deeds.

When feeling overwhelmed,
I find that looking ahead is only helpful
when it comes to making sure that
I have enough panty hose without runs.
Otherwise, I cope in the moment better
if I don't worry about the future.
Breathe.
Relax!

To-do lists. Planning ahead. Admonitions to be organized. For me, the most helpful way to live is to prepare for the basics (panty hose, for example) and then let go and live in the moment. Energy directed to worrying about what might happen depletes reserves for the future.

Creativity

Barbara Cook, as quoted by Charles Isherwood, "Take Off Your Emotional Clothes and Sing," *New York Times,* December 11, 2005

Barbara Cook (1927–) is recognized as a premier interpreter of Broadway songs and standards. As a young performer, she was lauded for her lyric soprano voice. In middle age, a transition was required, and she began a celebrated second career as a cabaret and concert singer. Now in her 80s, she still continues to win rave reviews.

One-time critic for *Variety,* Charles Isherwood became a theatre critic for the *New York Times* in 2004. Here is Mr. Isherwood on Ms. Cook's advice: "Plain but potent words, and not just applicable to performers… When performers first step onstage, they may be looking for approbation in the form of nourishing applause. But [Ms. Cook's lesson is] that artists achieve their peak when they learn to stop proving themselves and simply, to borrow the Shakespearean phrase, 'let be.' It's their humanity we respond to in the end, their ability to strip away the self-consciousness that locks us inside ourselves, and reveals the stuff that boils in our souls. Talent is necessary, training is important, but they'll only get you halfway to becoming a real artist."

Your own humanity is your pathway to artistry…
We have to find the courage to take off our emotional clothes…
We feel we're not enough, that the world doesn't want us…
The place that seems most dangerous is exactly where safety lies.

—Singer and actress Barbara Cook's advice to students in a Juilliard master class

Let be who you are. Allowing oneself to be exposed can be an act of self-discovery.

Part of talent is a willingness to work hard at it.
Without that part, not much will be accomplished.

—My father

It may be years before a writer's "first" novel is taken up by reviewers and a new "voice" is recognized. And painters may work unrecognized for years, accumulating canvasses, before "discovery." Talent is just the beginning; it is dedication and commitment that lead to its realization.

Work.

You can't keep it up all the time.
On the other hand,
deliberate work,
nibbling away at a project,
can accomplish more than you think.
Showing up each day and
doing something
may be better
than waiting for inspiration.

When I feel inspired, I try to seize the moment. But what if I don't feel motivated? As I grow older, I am learning how much the deliberateness and discipline of keeping at a project brings its own inspiration.

Kitty Pechet is a calligraphic artist, competitive surfer, wife, mother, grandmother, friend. She is also a "creativity coach," who has a gift for encouraging her students, and often does so, by writing notes addressed to our "inner artist."

Go see or hear something.
Consider the underlying meaning,
rather than style, popularity, technique, or surface.
Search for emotion, politics, passions, spiritual quality
or whatever is there.

—Kitty Pechet

Responding to a painting, music or some other creative work is a way to reflect on our own lives. Our response can open an inner dialogue. There are times when just "being" with one's response, rather than analyzing it, is the gift of the art. I studied art and music through school and college; my husband didn't. But when we go to a museum or attend a concert or ballet, his observations often make me see a work with new eyes.

How has the year in arts and creativity been for you?
Where have you been and where are you going?
Have you a plan?
Do you need a buddy for mutual support?
As you think, visualize geography;
amazing creations are based in geography.
Think about mountaintops, music, and mystics.
As a starter, where are you and where will you be?

—Kitty Pechet, Note to students

Kitty Pechet's course on the creative process invites her students to express themselves in ways they might not discover on their own.

When I joined Kitty's class, each student was working on a different project. Some were writing, others sketched. One person arranged small, smooth stones during class, and then put them back into containers at the end of each session. Another woman was editing her mother's diary. Yet another focused on Japanese calligraphy. And everyone encouraged each other. The variety of projects and supportive atmosphere encouraged me to explore my own ideas without worrying about the final product. The open-endedness was freeing.

Artists know that negative space
defines a composition.
Musicians know that the
silence between notes
is as much a part of the
experience of the music as the notes.
Think of space and silence
when you breathe,
knowing that the pause
between the in-breath
and the out-breath
fills you.

Paying attention to one's breath is a reminder of how full of life we are. Imagine soothing oxygen, filling your body, reaching every cell. It is a way to stay in the moment.

G.K. Chesterton, *What's Wrong with the World* (New York: Dodd, Mead and Company, 1910), p. 320.

G.K. (Gilbert Keith) Chesterton (1874–1936) offered this reflection twice in his writings. The first occasion was in *What's Wrong with the World,* a book-length response to the question issued by the (London) *Times.* The book touches on many subjects, but the quotation at hand comes at the end of the chapter on education, specifically regarding the superiority of an amateur teacher, a mother, in pouring the wonder of the universe into her child. Later, humorously, Chesterton, quoted himself in "When Doctors Agree," a detective story in the posthumously published, *The Paradoxes of Mr. Pond* (1937) His appropriation of his own quotation is made in a defense of hobbies, amateurs and general duffers. This version is, with a minor change, "If a thing is worth doing, it is worth doing badly."

Chesterton was one of the best-known English political and religious thinkers of his time, famous for making points by way of aphorism and paradox. A journalist and opinion columnist as a young man, he went on to produce a voluminous output of popular detective fiction (the Father Brown mysteries), poetry, plays, and biography. It is said that he began writing to find his way out of depression and found his faith. As a committed Christian, he engaged in notably amicable public debate with opponents such as Bertrand Russell, H.G. Wells, and George Bernard Shaw. (It was Chesterton who suggested, "If there were no God, there would be no atheists.") Although Chesterton is not read so much today, the list of later writers influenced by him is astonishingly long and diverse, including C.S. Lewis, Graham Greene, Evelyn Waugh, Jorge Luis Borges, Gabriel García Marquez, Dorothy Sayers, Agatha Christie, George Orwell, Franz Kafka, and Ingmar Bergman, among many others.

...if a thing is worth doing,
it is worth doing badly.

—G.K. Chesterton

My seven-year-old granddaughter came back from camp and said she was learning to make mosaic pictures and hers didn't turn out the way she hoped. The teacher counseled, "There are no mistakes in art," so my granddaughter happily readjusted her expectations and began enjoying mosaic-making. What my granddaughter learned underscores Chesterton's wisdom—there are things worth doing on one's own, even if the results are not "professional."

Nkosi Johnson, an 11-year-old South African boy with AIDS, as quoted by ABC reporter, Jim Wooten, in an interview with Michele Norris on NPR's *All Things Considered,* December 1, 2004

Nkosi Johnson inspired people around the world to action in the fight against the AIDS epidemic when he spoke at an international conference in Durban in 2000. Born into poverty in a province hit hard by the HIV virus, Nkosi was the longest surviving child with AIDS in South Africa at the time he died at age 12. His courage in the face of death is profiled in Jim Wooten's book, *We Are All the Same: A Story of a Boy's Courage and a Mother's Love* (New York: Penguin Press, 2004).

Do all you can
with what you have
in the time you have,
in the place you are.

—Nkosi Johnson

Nikosi told Jim Wooten that, even though he didn't want to die, he was not afraid of dying. It was then that he gave this philosophy of life. It is moving to think of a child composing and living these words.

SARK, aka Susan Ariel Rainbow Kennedy, *Living Juicy: Daily Morsels for Your Creative Soul* (Berkley, California: Celestial Arts/Ten Speed Press, 1994), April 9

SARK's talents include a gift for choosing evocative book titles. Samples include *Succulent Wild Woman, The Bodacious Book of Succulence,* and *Eat Mangoes Naked.*

Expression is the opposite of de-pression.
Whenever we de-press, we usually need to express.
Tune your channel to creativity and let the goodness flow out of you.

—SARK, aka Susan Ariel Rainbow Kennedy

Expressions can take many forms—singing in the shower, dancing in the kitchen, photographing or sketching a flower in your garden, experimenting with a favorite recipe.

Mihaly Csikszentmihalyi, *The Evolving Self: A Psychology for the Third Millennium* (New York: Harper Collins Publishers, 1993), p. xiii

A leading researcher on positive psychology, Mihaly Csikszentmihalyi (1934–) began his study of happiness five decades ago as a doctoral student at the University of Chicago. His topic: creativity and how creative people identify questions that no one has addressed before. Professor Csikszentmihalyi's observation of artists at work led him to the notion of "flow," and his own life work.

Some things are just fun to do....
The obvious question is, Why are these things fun?
...I called it "flow"...
a metaphor...for being carried away by a current,
everything moving smoothly without effort.
Contrary to expectation, "flow" usually happens not during relaxing
moments of leisure and entertainment, but rather when we are actively
involved in a difficult enterprise,
in a task that stretches our physical or mental abilities.
...when challenges are high and personal skills are used to the utmost,
we experience this rare state of consciousness.

—Mihaly Csikszentmihalyi

Why do some people love their work, and even liken it to play? The answer lies in their ability to engage in an activity—any activity—that is involving, demanding of concentration, absorbing of body and mind. To Professor Csikszentmihalyi, the sense of "flow" that results looks as close to happiness as might be imagined.

Herbert Benson and William Proctor, *The Breakout Principle: How to Activate the Natural Trigger That Maximizes Creativity, Athletic Performance, Productivity and Personal Well-Being* (New York: Schribner, 2003), pp. xi–xii

Trained as a cardiologist, Herbert Benson (1935–) was an early leader in mind/body medicine and research. In 1975, Dr. Benson coined a name—the Relaxation Response—to describe our ability to counteract the fight or flight response aroused by an adrenaline surge. More recently, he introduced another term into the self-help lexicon—the Breakout Principle—the idea that relaxation—a break in mental patterns—can allow us to make a transition to heightened performance and insight. Dr. Benson presents evidence that a period of relaxation after intense work can lead to a creative breakthrough, whatever the focus of one's effort—intellectual, athletic, spiritual.

Breakouts

…may be triggered by traditional relaxation-response techniques,
such as silently repeating a word, prayer, or phrase—
or engaging in a repetitive physical activity—
while assuming a passive attitude.

—Herbert Benson and William Proctor

Herbert Benson's research on enhancing performance reminds me to avail myself of the benefits of taking a break after I have been working on a project for a sustained period of time. The result might just be a creative leap! Even if I don't experience an epiphany, I have relaxed, renewed my energy and perspective, and maybe avoided one of those moments when the stress of one project bubbles over to affect other projects and people.

Creativity

A Creativity Exercise

Gather some of your favorite art materials, something easy. Magic markers in various colors, pencils, crayons, colored paper, large paper or tape together several pieces of smaller paper for your starting place. You will use two large pieces. Gather stickers, scissors, glue or tape. You might go through magazines or newspapers and tear out pages that appeal to you for one reason or another. Don't analyze your choices. Just respond to your instinct.

On the next page are two columns—"Roles in My Life" and "Characteristics of My Life." Check the ones that apply and add if there are other roles or characteristics.

After checking or circling the lists, take some time to contemplate the large blank piece of paper. Consider how you might represent the way your life is now. You can do so as simply as drawing a circle and marking off the amounts of time you spend in one role in one place. I invite you to let go and be creative, like you were in kindergarten. Make your creation simple or complex. Just have fun with it.

When you have finished, consider what your artwork tells you. Write it out or talk to a friend or family member about what you have discovered.

Next, take the other larger piece of paper and look at your lists and see if there are other roles and characteristics you wish to add to make a design for your future which could be next week, next year or longer term.

Look at the second blank piece of paper. Begin responding to the lists and the art materials and create a mosaic or quilt to give you a future to think about.

When you are finished, write about what you experienced and what your finished work reflects. Or talk with someone.

Put the finished pieces on your refrigerator or mirror so that you look at them everyday. They can also be used in talking with someone about your needs and desires to reallocate your time and the way you live.

Roles I Play	Characteristics of My Life
Daughter/Son	School
Friend	Home
Girlfriend/Boyfriend	Family
Student	Vacation
Worker	Work
Volunteer	Hobbies
Sister/Brother	City
Roommate	Country
Mother/Father	Spirituality
Wife/Husband	Exercise
	Sports
	Indoors
	Outdoors
	Sleep

Add your own suggestions.

I developed this exercise many years ago for my work with people in life transitions. Individually or in groups, my "students" have produced amazing creations—from simple pen drawings on paper to three-dimensional constructions.

Sue Monk Kidd, *When the Heart Waits: Spiritual Direction for Life's Sacred Questions* (New York: HarperCollins, 1990), p. 128

Waiting for spiritual transformation and feeling unable to pray, Sue Monk Kidd describes how she came to look for God within herself.

The prayer she was looking for was not about asking, but emptying and letting God flow in. Recalling a T.S. Eliot poem, she began to think in terms of a "still point"—a spiritual place that we must all find in our own way.

Sue Monk Kidd gave me the image of stillness that can heal, and powerfully so when it is shared. As for Meister Eckhart and Brother Steindl-Rast, what a difference 600 years makes!

I believe in the individuality of each human soul.
We're each artists, along with God, in its creation.
Meister Eckhart* believed that an artist isn't a special kind of person
but that each person is a special kind of artist.
Think of it; you're your own special kind of artist.
Your soul is your canvas, your flute, your poem.
And you paint it, play it, and write it as every true artist does—
in unique collaboration with God.
[Our individuality] makes for diversity
in our approaches to the still point.
What then binds those approaches?
A deep intent of the whole heart to God.
David Steindl-Rast** says that anything we do
with a whole heart can be prayer.
In wholeheartedness, our entire being is united in its aim toward God,
toward the deep Center within.
You have found and will find your own ways of doing this.

—Sue Monk Kidd

* Eckhart von Hochheim (c. 1260–c. 1328) was a German theologian, philosopher and mystic. A member of the Dominican Order of Preacher Friars, he sought in his sermons to inspire his listeners to do good. Accused of straying from orthodox language, he was tried for heresy and gave defense against any heretical intent that is a theological classic. Meister Eckhart disappeared from the public arena before a papal verdict was rendered. Whether he died or continued his ministry in anonymity is not known.

** A Benedictine, Brother David Steindl-Rast is an Austrian-American Roman Catholic theologian, known for engaging in interfaith dialogue and work on the interaction between spirituality and science. Indeed, he received Vatican approval for his outreach.

Creativity

How do you make things show up in a painting?
It isn't a matter of being right, but what works.

These words are from Kitty Pechet, who is a natural at giving insights from her own creative process. In one class, I was laboring over some flowers. Finally, the colors were "right," but you couldn't see them in the painting. As Kitty pointed out, inaccurate colors often give the right impression. A painting is like a play with a set of characters (in this case, flowers) speaking their parts on stage. Sometimes improvisation makes the play come alive.

Visualizations

Visualizations

Visualizations are a kind of meditation.
First, find a comfortable, quiet place.
Then pay attention to your breathing.
Note the coolness of the In-Breath, and
the warmth of the Out-Breath,
whether from your mouth or nose.

When you can feel yourself beginning to relax,
use one of the visualizations that follow
or create your own.

Visualization

Think about lying on your back.
Observe the clouds.
Some are grey, filled with rain;
others are white, billowing, playfully changing forms.
All move with the wind.
Some race across the sky;
others proceed slowly, almost imperceptibly.

Observe.
Don't attach.
Let go.
Breathe,
in,
out.

Visualization

Imagine
looking out to sea.

There is a
sailboat.

Is it riding along the waves
gently,
running with the wind?

Or is it beating into the wind,
heeling sharply, crew hiked out?

Does your imagined sailboat
reflect your life right now?

Is God, the Wind Blower, asking you
to make some slight adjustments
or must you find a course?

Breathe,
in,
out.

Visualization

With wireless communications,
the image of an umbilical telephone cord
is becoming an anachronism.
Still, I think of all the times when I have
connected with my children
and the telephone cord has felt like
an extended umbilical cord.

The real cord may have been cut,
but the connection remains.

Visualization

I feel called to
bring my light
to the world.
But
sometimes it feels like
a strong wind is
trying to blow my light out.
At these times, I see
a hurricane lamp
protecting the light and
letting it shine.

Be there.
Be safe.

Visualization

During meditation,
I have learned that if you ask yourself
how deeply you are engaged,
the answer
comes clearly,
one to ten.

Visualization

When I want to check
my thermometer of energy
in a quiet state
I assess where I am,
one to ten.

Visualization

Are you carrying a lot on your shoulders?

Assume a quiet state of mind.
Think of a pack on your back.
What is in the pack?
What is making it too heavy to carry?
See yourself
removing that weight from the pack.
How does it feel now?
Do you need to remove more weights from the pack
so that you can carry it?
How do you feel now?

Sometimes we don't know
how much we are carrying
until we lighten the load.

Visualization

Do you feel like a
spring
wound too tightly?
As you begin to unwind,
do you realize that there is even
more tension
than you were aware?

Try to release the tension.
Breathe,
in,
out.

Visualization

Do you like to have the cushions
all fluffed up?
Or,
do you enjoy having
family and friends enjoy
those soft cushions,
even if the cushion display is a bit messy?

Visualization

Are you facing a transition?

Transitions require adjustments,
but there are rewards
to be discovered in new places
and new people.
Still, there is anxiety along with the adventure.

What can you hold onto
as you make the transition?

Visualization

Are you the kind of person
who stands on the side of the pool,
hesitant to jump in?
Can you see yourself, in the next frame,
going off the diving board,
jumping with great joy?

Genes may make some of us hesitant by nature.
Though we may pause before a challenge,
we can move forward, embrace life,
and jump in.

My Meditation Healing Ritual

With my hands on my head,
I say, "Lord, heal my mind so that I may think clearly."
With my hands on my eyes,
"Lord, heal my eyes,
so that I may see others with compassion and myself as well."
With my hands on my ears,
"Lord, let me hear and truly listen."
With my hands on my throat,
"Lord, may I speak the truth and know when to be quiet."
With hands on heart,
"Lord, may I be more open to your love."
Holding lower abdomen,
"Lord, let me let go of what I don't need anymore.
Let it be released by the power of your love so I may reflect Your Light
more clearly."

*It helps me to breathe and pause at each line of this visualization prayer. I don't change
the words, but I find that I do change the way I say them or turn them over in my mind,
sometimes lingering longer at one part or another, taking an extra breath or two. I do so
in compassion for myself, as I quietly release what I don't need anymore.*

Living Lines

Mind, Body, Spirit

Even on a difficult day, it is possible to find "delight."
I was reintroduced to the word "delight"
by Brother Curtis of the Society of St. John the Evangelist,
when he spoke of his "delight" at an upcoming sabbatical.
The source of his "delight"?
Simply the opportunity TO BE.

As suggested by Brother Curtis, "delight" may be taken in a simple quiet moment.
With enough "delights," perhaps we can take a mini-sabbatical without leaving the
house. I like to imagine lighting the dark by connecting dots of "delight."

Things bubble up to the surface
when it is safe to deal with them.

That safe time can be
months, years, a lifetime later.

Safe doesn't mean easy.

Life's choices produce a constant stream of second thoughts, worries, and regrets. We may not be aware of what is floating below the surface until some event brings a forgotten memory to our consciousness. We all experience moments of reckoning when we must stop and readdress the past. Several years ago, my health led me to a deep immersion in unresolved conflicts as far back as early childhood. It was a safe time to look back, but it was not easy.

SARK (aka Susan Ariel Rainbow Kennedy), *Living Juicy: Daily Morsels for Your Creative Soul* (Berkeley, California: Celestial Arts/Ten Speed Press, 1994), February 27

Upon first encounter, SARK's *Living Juicy* may impress the reader as cute, fun for the occasional flip-through, but her "morsels" have inspirational staying power. SARK was one of the women featured on the PBS series, *Women of Wisdom and Power.*

You can heal
what you're able to feel.

—SARK (aka Susan Ariel Rainbow Kennedy)

I have learned that to heal deeply, I must be conscious of my feelings—no matter how painful, whether old wounds or fresh ones.

Rose Tremain (1941–) is a British novelist, whose books often dramatize a moment of truth in the lives of lonely outsiders. Her aphorism reportedly made its first appearance in a newspaper column in 1989. It has circulated so widely since then that many people quote it, but have no idea whose words they are using. More recently, Ms. Tremain responded to a call to noted authors by the *Guardian* on the subject of the golden rules that they bring to their writing practice. Two of her rules struck me, "Never be satisfied with a first draft" and "When an idea comes, spend silent time with it."

Living Lines

Life is not a dress rehearsal.

—Aphorism widely attributed to Rose Tremain

There are different approaches to healing, but whether we have help or work alone, we have to be fully immersed in the process. Our will to heal, our will to live, is up to us.

I am always surprised when I experience
a delayed reaction after a challenging time.
Sometimes part of the surprise is
how long the delay may be.

Another part of the surprise may be the abruptness of the reaction.

Turbulence.

Sometimes a plane flight is smooth sailing all the way,
and our thoughts wander pleasantly.
On other flights, the plane may be buffeted by turbulence.
Muscles tense and fear threatens thought.

When I feel inner turbulence, I try to release the tension in my body and in my mind. Reducing the resistance of muscle and thought, the turbulence eases. My experience has given me great respect for the power of breathing. What a wonderful gift our breath is! We can monitor our stress level by observing how deeply we are breathing (or holding our breath). By paying attention we can use our breath to change our body's reaction to stress.

A founding figure in Western philosophy, Aristotle (384 B.C.E.—322 B.C.E.) established a philosophical system that encompassed morality and aesthetics, logic and science, politics and metaphysics. A student of Plato and teacher of Alexander the Great, Aristotle came as close as any man in history to knowing everything that was to be known in his own time. Of his theory concerning the connection between body and soul, it is interesting to note that this subject would have engaged Aristotle even as a boy for his father was the court physician to the king of Macedon.

Soul and body, I suggest, react sympathetically upon each other;
a change in the state of the soul produces
a change in the shape of the body,
and conversely:
a change in the shape of the body produces
a change in the state of the soul.

—Aristotle, *Physiognomics,* c. 350 B.C.E

Aristotle's theory is much quoted by therapists today. It is humbling to think that the ancient Greeks framed questions that still preoccupy us more than 23 centuries later. Yet, it is exciting, too, because over the past two decades, scientists have acquired powerful new imaging tools that are revolutionizing our understanding of the connection between body and mind.

His Holiness the Dalai Lama and Howard C. Cutler, M.D., *The Art of Happiness: A Handbook for Living* (New York: Riverhead Books, A Member of Penguin Group (USA) Inc., 1998), pp. 13–14

His Holiness the Fourteenth Dalai Lama, Tenzin Gyatso (1935–), is the spiritual leader of Tibet, recognized at the age of two as the reincarnation of the 13th Dalai Lama. Tibetans believe that the Dalai Lama is the manifestation of the Bodhisattva of Compassion, the patron saint of Tibet. (Bodhisattvas are enlightened beings who have postponed their own nirvana and chosen rebirth in order to serve humanity.) The Dalai Lama's monastic education began at the age of six and continued to the Tibetan equivalent of a doctoral degree in Buddhist philosophy, even as he assumed political leadership of Tibet at age 15. Since fleeing Chinese suppression in 1959, he has made his home at Dharamsala in northern India. Although the Dalai Lama has devoted his life to nonviolent struggle for the liberation of Tibet (winning the Nobel Peace Prize in 1989), he is also keenly interested in Western science, and has dedicated himself to encouraging scientists to examine Buddhist spiritual practice. He has undertaken this work, not in an attempt to win converts to Buddhism, but in the hope of benefiting society in general.

Howard Cutler is an American psychiatrist who has devoted a career to "happiness," an interest that grew out of a small grant for the study of traditional Tibetan medicine. From the time of his first meeting with the Dalai Lama in 1982, the Tibetan leader never impressed him as less than a genuinely happy person—contented despite great responsibilities and personal sacrifices. This palpable happiness made the young American psychiatrist curious to understand the Dalai Lama's approach to living and meditation.

Although the Dalai Lama had written scholarly books on Buddhism, he had never addressed a Western audience on living a happy everyday life. Even with the publicity surrounding the Dalai Lama's Nobel Peace Prize, the general public had little sense of him as a person. Dr. Cutler thus proposed the idea of a book to the Dalai Lama; to his surprise, the Tibetan spiritual leader readily said "yes." Though the collaboration went smoothly, Dr. Cutler did not foresee the difficulty of finding a mainstream publisher for a book based on conversations about happiness. Indeed, it was five years before a publisher was found, and this, thanks partly to the serendipity of a chance meeting on a New York subway. From a small first printing in 1998, *The Art of Happiness* took a place on the New York Times bestseller list, where it stayed for two years and has gained a place in the popular culture.

From a Dialogue between the Dalai Lama
and a Western-Trained Psychiatrist

I believe that the very purpose of our life is to seek happiness. That is clear. Whether one believes in religion or not whether one believes in this religion or that religion, we all are seeking something better in life. So, I think, the very motion of our life is towards happiness...

With these words, spoken before a large audience in Arizona, the Dalai Lama cut to the heart of his message. But his claim that the purpose of life was happiness raised a question in my mind. Later when we were alone, I asked, "Are *you* happy?"

"Yes," he said. He paused, then added, "Yes...definitely." There was a quiet sincerity in his voice that left no doubt— a sincerity that was reflected in his expression and in his eyes.

"But is happiness a reasonable goal for most of us?" I asked." Is it really possible?"
"Yes.
I believe that happiness can be achieved through training the mind."

—His Holiness the Dalia Lama and Howard C. Cutler, M.D.

The Dalai Lama is known for his ready smile. A key to happiness?

Mind, Body, Spirit

Richard Davidson as quoted by Daniel Goleman in "The Lama in the Lab," *Destructive Emotions: How Can We Overcome Them, A Scientific Dialogue with the Dalai Lama* (New York: Bantam Dell, A Division of Random House, Inc., 2003), p. 25

Daniel Goleman, the "narrator" of the 2000 Mind and Life Institute conference on "Destructive Emotions," takes the reader into the world of brain imaging at University of Wisconsin's Laboratory for Affective Neuroscience. There, he recreates a very particular experimental session arranged by the lab's director, neuroscientist Richard Davidson. Nearly a decade before, Professor Davidson had been invited by the Dalai Lama to Dharamsala to interview monks with extensive mediation experience. A decade later, the professor returned the favor with an invitation to his own lab.

One special invitee was a Buddhist monk with an unusual background—a highly skilled meditator and Western convert to Buddhism, who had trained in the Himalayas for more than three decades, including years with one of Tibet's spiritual masters. Tibetan Buddhism offers perhaps more meditation methods than any contemplative tradition, so this monk was a special guest indeed.

With Functional Magnetic Resonance Imaging (fMRI) and other imaging techniques, Professor Davidson's research team proposed analyzing the monk's brain activity associated with three meditative states—visualization, one-pointed concentration, and generating compassion. The Western monk proposed three more—meditations on devotion, fearlessness, and an open state. This latter state he described as one of "thought-free wakefulness" where the mind is "open, vast and aware, with no intentional mental activity…not focused on anything, yet totally present." (p. 6) The monk showed strong shifts in imaging signals with each meditative state. A dramatic finding because control subjects show such shifts only between waking and sleeping.

Living Lines

[The brain] can be trained because the very structure of
our brain can be modified...
We now have the methods
to show how the brain changes with [meditation practices],
and how our mental and physical health
may improve as a consequence.

—Richard Davidson

Professor Davidson's research has provided evidence that meditation can shift the brain as well as the body. If brain structure can be changed, it is possible that different forms of meditation can be used to change the circuitry in the brain associated with different aspects of emotion. In other words, neuroscience can lead to the identification of new connections that might allow effective regulation of distressing emotions, such as anxiety, fear and anger.

His Holiness the Dalai Lama, "Preface to the 10th Anniversary Edition," *The Art of Happiness: A Handbook for Living* (New York: Riverhead Books, A Member of Penguin Group (USA) Inc., 2009), p. xii

Initial sales expectations for *The Art of Happiness* were modest, but awareness spread fast by word of mouth. The Dalai Lama and Dr. Cutler subsequently published two companion books, *The Art of Happiness at Work* (2003) and *The Art of Happiness in a Troubled World* (2009), as well as a 10th anniversary edition of the original book with expanded preface and introduction.

The Dalai Lama began a dialogue with Western scientists in 1973, the year of his first time to the West. In the 1980s, he created a structure for these conversations with the founding of the Mind and Life Institute, a nonprofit organization dedicated to exploring the relationship of Western science and Buddhist tradition. Each approach— science and Buddhism—is dedicated to understanding the nature of reality and promoting human wellbeing. The Dalai Lama's stated goal is not to further Buddhism, but to see where Buddhist tradition may benefit society, outside of the religious realm.

One of the Institute's goals is to sponsor high-level scientific research on meditation and the mind, and thereby contribute to medicine, neuroscience, psychology, education, and ultimately the welfare of mankind. Since 1987, the Institute has encouraged scientific research through regular conferences on a variety of subjects at the intersection of Buddhism, the cognitive sciences, and neuroscience. These conferences have made an impact on the world of academic science, but attendance is necessarily limited. Accordingly, the Dalai Lama has thus sought a wider audience for the implications of these exchanges through a full travel schedule of public conferences and talks, with follow-up books published at regular intervals.

Living Lines

Today, with new insights from the field of neuroscience,
especially with the discovery of brain plasticity,
we know that the human brain is highly amenable
to change and adaptation,
even at advanced ages, as in one's seventies, as I am now.
The revered thirteenth-century Tibetan master
Skaya Pandita once said,
"Seek learning even if you were to die tomorrow."

—His Holiness the Dalai Lama

With obvious satisfaction and economy of words, the Dalai Lama points to the convergence between modern science and ancient Buddhist teaching with the discovery of brain plasticity—that brain structure may be modified well into adulthood. How can we find greater happiness and so overcome life's inevitable troubles and suffering? The Dalai Lama believes that the answer can be found in our own inner resources. The idea of training the mind has been central to Buddhism for 2,500 years. Western scientists are now paying attention.

Sharon Begley, *Train Your Mind, Change Your Brain: How a New Science Reveals Our Extraordinary Potential to Transform Ourselves* (New York: Ballantine Books, An Imprint of the Random House Publishing Group, 2007), p. 254

Science journalist Sharon Begley is well known to readers of the *Wall Street Journal* and *Newsweek*. In *Train Your Mind,* she addresses not just how perception or physical training affects the brain, but the evidence that *thought* itself can change neural architecture. Thanks to an invitation from the Mind and Life Institute, she had a front-row seat at the Dalai Lama's 2004 conference of Buddhist scholars and monks and Western neuroscientists. The resulting book takes readers from the foundational questions of neuroscience right up to research on its frontiers. Findings that the brain is endowed with the ability to change—that it is characterized by "neuroplasticity"—has enormous implications, not just for those seeking to recover from stroke or psychiatric disease, but for all of us as we confront the challenges of life.

The conscious act of thinking about one's thoughts
in a different way
changes the very brain circuits
that do that thinking…
Such willfully induced brain changes
require focus, training, and effort,
but a growing number of studies using neuroimaging show
how real these changes are.
They come from within.
As the discoveries of…this self-directed neuroplasticity,
trickle down to clinics and schools and plain old living rooms,
the ability to willfully change the brain
will become a central part of our lives—
and our understanding of what it means to be human.

—Sharon Begley

The discovery that mere thought can alter the brain is astonishing. Recent neuroscience findings have motivated me to be even more diligent in my meditation practice!

Sandra Blakeslee and Matthew Blakeslee, *The Body Has a Mind of Its Own: How Body Maps in Your Brain Help You Do (Almost) Everything Better* (New York: Random House, 2008), p. 202

Veteran New York Times science writer Sandra Blakeslee and her son Matthew Blakeslee take readers to another frontier of neuroscience research. Their book explains how the brain "maps" areas of the body, as well as "peripersonal" space within arm's reach or leg swing. The brain even maps body space extenders—whether gardening tools, cars, trucks, cranes, or remotely operated medical devices.

Active, cultivated awareness
of your internal sensations
can lead to amazing results.
Experienced meditators like yogis and lamas
actually gain conscious control over
their heart rates,
oxygen consumption,
and other basic autonomic functions.
They also say they feel extremely happy and emotionally stable.
And just as a body builder
can point to his bulging muscles
as proof that he hits the gym regularly,
an experienced meditator shows structural brain changes reflecting
his long hours of breathing and mindfulness.

—Sandra Blakeslee and Matthew Blakeslee

The Blakeslees' book offers lots of small practical applications from safer walking for older people to increasing one's persuasiveness. As for the big picture, it offers the reader a new sense of what the authors call "me-ness"—the perception that the body and brain exist for each other.

Spirit Storage

Spirit Storage is the name of an acupuncture point on the upper chest.
At a time when I was challenged on many fronts to share my energy,
this acupuncture term reminded me to pay attention
to my reserves of spirit.

My personal image of Spirit Storage took a new form
when a dear friend gave me a gold, beaded journal.
This beautiful book is now my reminder that
my store of spirit energy is a precious resource.

The best way I have found of keeping track of my store of spiritual energy—spirit storage—is in meditation. In the quiet, I ask myself if I need to replenish my spirit supply. Sometimes, I realize that I had not been aware that my spirit energy was low.

Living Lines

Energy

Sometimes when I am tired,
I realize this weariness is the result of having given my energy to others.
Then, what I need is to give myself quiet to restore.

There are different ways to recover from fatigue. For me, it isn't always a matter of needing more sleep, but having enough quiet time to read, to think, to meditate, or just sit in a comfortable chair. Watching the patterns of leaves blowing in the wind, listening to chattering birds, feeling a cold breeze or the warmth of the sun—all have restorative power.

SARK (aka Susan Ariel Rainbow Kennedy), *Living Juicy: Daily Morsels for Your Creative Soul* (Berkeley, California: Celestial Arts/Ten Speed Press, 1994), February 7

SARK pushes her readers to make their creative dreams come true, and she shows the way with her own story. She is open about the fact that her own flaws—a tendency to procrastinate or to want perfection—sometimes slow her down, but not for long.

SARK's Living Juicy *is full of wonderful insights. I learned that I am an "extroverted introvert," which means that I enjoy being with people, but that I need quiet time to restore my energy.*

We can learn to energize others the more
we learn about energizing ourselves.
You know those "sparkle plenty" people?
Or the quiet type that projects big energy?
Either way, or in between, we can help others with our energy,
as long as we learn about grounding ourselves,
running energy and practicing self-care.
Sometimes I go out into the world and project "too much energy"
and return home drained and exhausted.
So I am learning how to pull my "energy antennas"
in and nourish myself first.
On airplanes, we are instructed to put on our own oxygen mask first
so we can better help a child.
Same thing—we must take care of ourselves first.

—SARK (aka Susan Ariel Rainbow Kennedy)

Mind, Body, Spirit

Trying to restore our emotional health
can be exhausting,
particularly if we have neglected it.
No wonder
people often choose to
numb their pain.

It takes courage and energy
to dig deep
and let emotional wounds heal.
We can heal only if we
know what the wounds are.

Our bodies hold onto emotional hurts, sometimes for years. There are many ways to help the healing process—prayer, meditation, yoga, reiki, and therapy—that strengthen the body along with the mind.

When you are sick or suffering a loss,
down physically, psychologically or spiritually,
you will know that recovery is around the corner
when you wake up in the morning
and that trouble is not your first thought.

When is "this" going to be over? Most of us have asked this question when we are sick or are experiencing a loss. I have not always been aware that the turning point has occurred until, one morning, I realize that "it" wasn't the first thing on my mind.

Mind, Body, Spirit

It is important
to take things slowly
and allow recovery to happen
at its own rate.

There are no magic formulas for healing physical, emotional and spiritual wounds. Healing occurs on its own schedule. Sometimes recovery can be traced in measurable milestones, and other times, it occurs quietly in the dark.

Placebo is a pharmacologically inert preparation
that may relieve symptoms through the power of suggestion.
I prefer Dr. Herbert Benson's definition,
"Remembered Wellness."

It helps to be aware of your feelings when you are well physically, emotionally and spiritually. Take them as a reference point. The memory of those feelings can guide you back to health when you are not so well.

Healing from the Inside Out

Wounds that heal superficially need deeper healing.
Sometimes the wound needs to be reopened to heal completely.

A friend, a nurse, helped a patient with a compound-fracture wound
that had become infected after the scar had formed.

She described how she cleaned the reopened wound daily.
Gradually, the festering cleared up and
the new healthy layers grew and sealed the wound.

My friend's ministries are a good metaphor for treating
psychological pain and emotional wounds. These wounds develop
a scab, then a scar, but may not heal deeply.

Some time later, sometimes more than once,
these wounds need to be reopened.
This reopening is very painful, but creates an
environment for deeper healing.

*I have thought of this metaphor many times and experienced the re-opening of
emotional wounds that needed to heal more deeply. At transition times in our lives, body
and spirit call out for a more intense exposure of our pain. Once the pain has been faced,
we can grow and thrive again.*

At the end of the day,
in the middle of the night,
after all the advice,
we have to figure it out for ourselves.

As a professional counselor, I sometimes find myself at the receiving end of my own advice. Even though I know what has worked for others, I still must take time to turn the problem over in my mind and find the right approach for me. How easy it is to give advice and how difficult it can be to take it!

Jon Kabat-Zinn, *Wherever You Go, There You Are, Mindfulness Meditation in Everyday Life* (New York: Hyperion, 1994), p. 195, 197, 198, 199

These lines condense the central message of Jon Kabat-Zinn's book.

Have you ever noticed that there is no running away from anything?
…ultimately you have to live the inner work yourself,
and that work always comes from the cloth of your own life…
There can be no resolution leading to growth
until the present situation has been faced completely and
you have opened to it with mindfulness,
allowing the roughness of the situation itself
to sand down your own rough edges.
In other words, you must be willing to let life itself
become your teacher…
So why not let go and admit that you might as well
be at home wherever you are?

—Jon Kabat-Zinn

Dr. Kabat-Zinn invites his readers to be in the moment, to be mindful to the core and so to heal. Whatever the unit of time—moment, hour, day—absorb it, learn from it.

Recovering,
physically and emotionally,
is not a straight line,
but a rolling up and down
in an upward direction.

Whether we are recovering physically, emotionally or both, it is easy to become discouraged if each day doesn't bring continuous improvement. Being patient with one's progress—knowing and accepting that there will naturally be ups and downs—is key to staying optimistic over the long haul.

When I asked a friend
whose husband had been very ill
how they were doing since he recovered,
she answered that they were in
post-traumatic bliss.

After the intensity of serious illness, the energy that had been expended in worry can explode into gratefulness and relief.

Thich Nhat Hanh, *The Miracle of Mindfulness* (Boston: Beacon Press, 1975), pp. 7–8

Thich Nhat Hanh is an expatriate Vietnamese Zen Buddhist monk. ("Thich" is a title used by Vietnamese monks and nuns that indicates they belong to a particular Buddhist clan.) An important figure in the development of Western Buddhism, Hanh has introduced mindfulness practices suited to Western sensibilities. His book, *The Miracle of Mindfulness,* is a manual on meditation. Hanh suggests that we treat our everyday activities as opportunities for being aware. From this perspective, it is clear that meditation is not meant to be an escape from reality, but a path to an increased awareness of reality.

Living Lines

When walking, the practitioner must be conscious that he is walking.
When sitting, the practitioner must be conscious that he is sitting.
When lying down, the practitioner must be conscious
that he is lying down.
No matter what position one's body is in,
the practitioner must be conscious of the position.
Practicing thus, the practitioner lives in direct and constant
mindfulness of the body.
The mindfulness of the positions of one's body is not enough.
We must be conscious of each breath,
each movement, every thought and feeling,
everything [that] has any relation to ourselves.

—Thich Nhat Hanh

If you would like to pursue the practice of meditation, I commend Thich Nhat Hanh's writings.

Dance as though no one is watching you.

—Anonymous advice on carved sign that I found on vacation

I love to dance, especially when no one is watching, so I bought the sign, and mounted it over our breakfast table when we returned home. I still look at it each morning, and do a little shuffle as I make breakfast. It never fails to make me smile.

Some time later, I found that my sign's wonderful advice is actually the first line of a quatrain (also anonymous):

> *Dance as though no one is watching.*
> *Love as though you've never been hurt before.*
> *Sing as though no one can hear you.*
> *Live as though heaven is on earth.*

"Ten seconds on your lip,
ten years on your hips,"
says my husband gleefully
as he pops a piece of chocolate into his mouth.

This little ditty comes to mind when I am tempted by some rich delight. At these moments, the concept of mindfulness is most helpful. Facing temptation, I take 10 seconds and ask myself if I really, really, really want that indulgence. Sometimes, the craving diminishes and my hips are saved from that extra weight. If I go ahead, I savor what whatever it is that I really, really wanted.

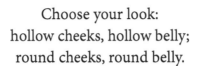

Choose your look:
hollow cheeks, hollow belly;
round cheeks, round belly.

—Advice from my first woman doctor

I received this advice when I was approaching 50. Years later, I seem to have "chosen" the "round" option, if it was in fact a choice. But I work—by regular exercising—to keep the rounded parts supported by strong muscles.

We often define courage as the end in itself.
But courage is about persevering
in spite of fear and the risks we see.
Courage is keeping at it,
even when we don't feel courageous.

Those whom we may admire for their courage may not actually feel courageous.
Perseverance may be the quality that they are cultivating.

Ralph Waldo Emerson, "Essay XII. Art,"
Essays: First Series, 1841

Descended from a seven-generation line of ministers, Ralph Waldo Emerson (1803–1882)—essayist, philosopher, poet—looked for God in nature, and by looking, sought to bring the Divine into his soul. Although it is said that he did not care for the label "transcendentalist," he was a leader of the New England group known by that name. A gifted speaker and an eloquent writer, Emerson had a way of minting aphorisms by connecting the ordinary with the philosophical. (An example, the command, "Go hitch your wagon to a star" is Emerson's.) Emerson insisted that his readers look at the world for themselves. In this, he remains modern, and his reflections certainly influenced many of the later philosophers whose words are included in this volume.

Though we travel the world over to find the beautiful,
we must carry it with us or we find it not.

—Ralph Waldo Emerson

Beauty can be found in the simplest and closest things. One October day, I was eating my lunch on the back deck and a red leaf floated onto my tray—a sign to look up. I sat there, enjoying the pleasure of eating outside and the show of fall colors. Crimson leaves fluttered in the slight breeze. Just then, my husband joined me with his lunch.

Thomas Merton, as quoted by Robert J. Wicks, *Seeds of Sensitivity* (Notre Dame, Indiana: Ave Maria Press, Inc., 1995), p. 104

Baptized an Anglican, Thomas Merton (1915–1968) became a Catholic in his early 20s, and a Trappist monk four years later. Merton's *The Seven Storey Mountain* is considered one of the best autobiographical books on faith ever written. Completed when Merton was only 31, it is a story of loss of security as a child, worldly youth and gradual spiritual awakening, conversion, and retreat to a monastic community in Kentucky. Although the Catholic faith that he embraced at the time of his conversion was one of extreme certainty, Merton became a proponent of interfaith dialogue. A prolific and gifted writer, Merton died in a tragic accident at the age of 53.

Courage comes and goes.
Hold on for the next supply.

—Thomas Merton

There are times when I "feel" courageous, and then become anxious that my courage may escape me. At such times, Thomas Merton's advice reassures that courage will return. G.K. Chesterton, quoted earlier, also gives perspective on courage, and with a touch of humor. Said Chesterton, "Courage is almost a contradiction is terms. It means a strong desire to live taking the form of a readiness to die." (Orthodoxy, 1908)

Mind, Body, Spirit

Czeslaw Milosz, first eight lines of "I Should Now," *Second Space: New Poems* (New York: HarperCollins Publishers, 2004), p. 21

Czeslaw Milosz (1911–2004) was a Polish émigré poet, novelist and essayist, 1980 Nobel laureate in Literature. A Catholic who witnessed the successive devastations of Nazi fascism and Soviet totalitarianism, Milosz's work explores questions of spiritual values at the same time that he gives thanks for life's beauty and sensual pleasures. Written after Milosz turned 90, the poems in *Second Space* are reflections on the poet's continued search for religious meaning. The lines quoted here are a wry commentary on aging. We like to think that we become wiser with age but who knows? Milosz admitted—directly and frankly—that his own "resolution" to be true was not always followed.

I should be wiser than I was.
Yet I don't know whether I am wiser.
Memory composes a story of shames and amazements.
The shames I closed inside myself, but the amazements,
at a sun-streak on a wall, at the trill of an oriole, a face,
an iris, a volume of poems, a person, endure and return in
　　brightness.
Such moments lifted me above my lameness.

—Czeslaw Milosz

I don't necessarily feel wiser as I age. However, I do remember coming upon similar challenges at earlier times and then hoping that what I learned before would help me. When I read Czeslaw Milosz's words, I was drawn into reflection on tests that may lie ahead. It is natural to assume that age will at least confer wisdom. But it is really a question of hoping that, when we are tested, we will remember—and act on—what we've learned from life's experiences.

What's Done Is Done.
Meaning, if you do it now,
it is done.
It can also mean,
get over it;
what's past is past.
Or it can mean, the past is over.
Learn.
Perhaps forgive.

"What's done is done"—in all its meanings—resonates with me and reminds me to focus on the present.

Spirituality

John O'Donohue, *Anam Ċara: A Book of Celtic Wisdom* (New York: Cliff Street Books, An Imprint of HarperCollins Publishers, 1997), p. xviii

An ordained priest who left the priesthood, John O'Donohue (1956–2008) was a native Gaelic speaker, poet and philosopher. O'Donohue's work calls on readers to see the treasure they have inherited in their own hearts. His 1997 bestseller, *Anam Ċara: A Book of Celtic Wisdom* is a meditation on Ireland's spiritual heritage. Those who knew O'Donohue's work were stunned when they learned of his sudden, unexpected death at age 52. Though he was totally committed to life, O'Donohue nonetheless saw death as a path to freedom. In "Reflection from Conamara" (published on his Website), he wrote [of those who are true to themselves], "...the view from your death bed will show a life of growth that gladdens the heart and takes away all the fear." O'Donohue's final book, published in 2008, was *To Bless the Space Between Us: A Book of Blessings*.

A note for non-Gaelic speakers: *Anam* is the Gaelic word for soul; *ċara* is the word for friend, so *anam ċara* means soul friend.

The body is your clay home,
your only home in the universe.
The body is in the soul;
this recognition
confers a sacred and mystical dignity on the body.

—John O'Donohue

John O'Donohue asks us to make a simple, but profound, shift in vision. Several years ago, I was introduced to O'Donohue's mystical and poetic vision at a concert of Irish music—harp-accompanied songs woven from ancient tales. The performing artist, Aine Minogue, expressed her belief that O'Donohue was inspired by the mystics of the Middle Ages—Hildegard of Bingen, Thomas Aquinas, and Meister Eckhart—who knew deep in their souls that the soul is where the body resides.

If we believe that the body is in the soul
and the soul is divine ground,
then the presence of the divine
is completely here,
close with us.

—John O'Donohue, *Anam Ċara*, p. 59

From his proposition that the body is in the soul, John O'Donohue offers this reflection for the reader's consideration: "Being in the soul, the body makes the senses thresholds of [one's own] soul."

The Celtic understanding did not set limitations of space or time on the soul. There is no cage for the soul. The soul is a divine light that flows into you and into your Other.

In everyone's life, there is great need for an *anam ċara*, a soul friend. In this love, you are understood as you are without mask or pretension. The superficial and functional lies and half-truths of social acquaintance fall away, you can be as you really are. Love allows understanding to dawn, and understanding is precious. Where you are understood, you are at home. Understanding nourishes belonging. When you really feel understood, you feel free to release yourself into the trust and shelter of the other person's soul.

—John O'Donohue, *Anam Ċara*, pp. 13–14

In Anam Ċara, *John O'Donohue explains that in the early Celtic church, a person who acted as a teacher, companion, or spiritual guide was called an* anam ċara—*"someone to whom you confessed, revealing the hidden intimacies of your life. With the* anam ċara *you could share your innermost self, your mind and your heart. This friendship was an act of recognition and belonging. When you had an* anam ċara, *your friendship cut across all convention, morality, and category."*

Frequently, in a journey of the soul,
the most precious moments are the mistakes.
They have brought you
to a place that you would otherwise
have always avoided.
You should bring a compassionate mindfulness
to your mistakes and wounds.

—John O'Donohue, *Anam Ċara*, p. 183

John O'Donohue was interviewed by Krista Tippet shortly before his death. That interview ended up being broadcast as a memorial in February 2008 on American Public Media's Speaking of Faith with Krista Tippet. *In the interview, this Irish mystic noted that we need something to push against in order to grow; a mistake can make us return to an inner place—an inner sanctuary, in O'Donohue's words—to rediscover our confidence and tranquility.*

Loving is
giving
what the person
needs,
not what you want to give.

Sometimes it takes time to learn what another person needs. That time is part of the gift.

Madeleine L'Engle, *The Irrational Season*
The Crosswicks Journal, Part 3 (New York:
HarperCollins Publishers), 1977), p. 123

Madeleine L'Engle (1918–2007) was the
author of the Newbury Medal–winning classic, *A Wrinkle in Time,* and many other popular books for children and adults. L'Engle
began writing as a girl and had published
several books by the time she was in her 20s.
Discouragement set in over the next decade,
and L'Engle was reportedly at the point of
giving up on writing when she had the inspiration for her masterpiece, *A Wrinkle in Time.*

An Episcopalian, L'Engle believed that her
fiction reflected her faith that the universe
has meaning. Still, her books—interwoven
with fantasy and myth—were controversial in
some religious quarters. Perhaps in answer to
this criticism, L'Engle wrote of her Christian
faith in several autobiographical books.
Testament to her faith was her long association with the Cathedral of St. John the Divine
in New York City, first as a volunteer librarian
and then as writer-in-residence.

[Some liken] the Holy Spirit to a shy and gentle bird
who must be approached quietly and slowly,
lest he be frightened and fly away.
[Others liken] the Holy Spirit to a ravening hawk...
my experiences have been more hawklike than dovelike.
But considerable violence is needed to pull my fragments together,
to join sunside and nightside;
it's a wildly athletic act to place the mind into the heart
and a lot of muscles get pulled.

—Madeleine L'Engle

Madeleine L'Engle begins this journal by sharing late-night, post-birthday thoughts, which turn to speculation about the nature of the universe. Recalling her familiar fictional voice, she offers a summary review of the theories of the creation of the universe and then a quick turn to memories of her children's questions (and her answers) on the subject. It strikes me that Ms. L'Engle was approximately the same age that I am now when she wrote this year-long journal. Like my other favorite authors, she shows that questioning—living with the questions—is strengthening and even provides some answers.

Brother Curtis Almquist, *Hope Abiding,*
newsletter of The Society of St. John the
Evangelist, Winter 2010

I have come to know Brother Curtis through services at the monastery of the Society of St. John the Evangelist. He delivered these reflections at a service of thanksgiving for an aged brother. Brother Curtis's homily was inspired by teachings of the Society's founder, Richard Meux Benson (1824–1915), who believed that God's glory manifested itself in the "brokenness" of our lives. In his homily, Brother Curtis explored this paradox, concluding that "The fruit of a life well lived is patience, humility, and then love."

Our own brokenness—
be it our lack of self-sufficiency,
our sense of inadequacy or incompleteness,
our own character flaws,
even our own despair—whatever it is,
our brokenness becomes
the portal in our own soul
where God breaks through to us.
…we have to be patient with life…
We were created in a state of imperfection, full of potential…
Patience does not preclude our suffering
but rather presumes it…
Growth is sometimes quite painful—growing pains…
That God will break through to us
in our brokenness
also invites the gift of humility.
Humility comes as a by-product of a well-lived life.
Humility is not something to work on
which would probably only produce its opposite, pride—
but rather something that simply evolves within our soul.

—Brother Curtis Almquist

Spirituality

My God is bigger
than the institutions
that try to contain Him/Her.

Each of us seeks a balance between dogma and free will, between religiosity and spirituality.

The butterfly
has long been a symbol of resurrection,
for as a caterpillar it disappears
into a protective cocoon,
and then emerges
on its own mysterious schedule,
transformed into a new creature,
beautiful and with the power of flight.

The butterfly as a symbol of patient transformation resonates with me. (Of course, I am not unique in my response to these beautiful, delicate creatures, or there wouldn't be so many butterfly exhibits at zoos and science museums.) In her book, When the Heart Waits, *Sue Monk Kidd, emphasizes the waiting in very personal terms: "We discover that the only way to achieve newness is to read our own obituary—to die to the old and open the door to the knock of waiting, to allow ourselves to be sheathed in the experience of incubating what needs to be born." (page 16) "Trust" in the process is the key.*

Trina Paulus, *Hope for the Flowers* (New York: Paulist Press, a Newman Book, 1972), p. 76

Trina Paulus wrote her book—after the upheavals of the 1960s—as a parable of hope. Still in print (more than two million copies) nearly 40 years later, it's a tale of two caterpillars, the intuitive Yellow (the female) and worried Stripe (the male), who learn that the only way to learn to fly is to surrender to the cocoon!

My copy of Trina Paulus's book is a first edition. As I double-checked the words of this reflection, I found a long-forgotten photograph that someone took of my husband and me outside of our church, standing in front of a Pancake Breakfast sign, painted yellow and striped.

"And if I decided to become a butterfly,"
said Yellow hesitantly. "What do I do?"
"Watch me. I'm making a cocoon.
"It looks like I'm hiding, I know,
but a cocoon is no escape.
"It's an in-between house where
the change takes place.
"It's a big step since you can
never return to caterpillar life.
"During the change, it will seem
to you or to anyone who might
peek that nothing is happening—
but the butterfly is already becoming.
"It just takes time!"

—Trina Paulus

Sue Monk Kidd, *When the Heart Waits: Spiritual Direction for Life's Sacred Questions* (New York: HarperCollins Publishers, 1990), p. 17

Here to further define "waiting," Sue Monk Kidd uses the word, "stayed-ness," coined by George Fox, 17th-century English Dissenter and founder of the Religious Society of Friends. (The story of Fox's own spiritual transformation—some viewed him as mad—in that dangerous century and place is quite remarkable.) Ms. Kidd suggests that in waiting, we will learn what is needed for transformation.

In the stayed-ness of waiting
we find everything we need in order to grow.
Suspended upside down in the heart of the question,
we touch the sacred spaces of real becoming.

—Sue Monk Kidd

I use the direct line
in talking to God,
not the party line.

In a world where we see so many versions of God in different religions, I seek a personal relationship with God.

Sometimes the list of people
to pray for is so long
that I end up sighing and saying,
"You know God."

Sometimes, I pray for someone or something in particular. Of all the people and causes in my heart, one or two people are usually at the top of my list. Holding the others in prayer without naming them, I am turning them over to God.

Robert Browning, "Bishop Blougram's Apology," 1855

Robert Browning (1812–1889), the English poet whose finest work was inspired by his courtship and marriage to Elizabeth Barrett, also addressed religious faith. In his approach to religion, Browning was strongly influenced by another woman—his mother, a staunch evangelical Christian. The poem cited here— "Bishop Blougram's Apology"—explores the question of faith in the form of a dialogue between a Catholic bishop whose belief is shaken occasionally by doubt and a literary man who does not disbelieve with absolute certainty.

The two lines on the facing page have stood on their own for over 100 years, published as a "gem" for thought and even in a teacher's guide as a "sentence sermon." In fact, Browning produced many notable aphorisms, many religious in nature. Two particularly familiar ones: "A man's reach should exceed his grasp, or what's a heaven for?" and "God's in his heaven, all's right with the world."

My business is not to remake myself.
But make the absolute best of what God made.

—Robert Browning

I've added another line to Robert Browning's job description—to discover God's purpose for me. And another of his lines from "Bishop Blougram's Apology" as well: "The aim, if reached or not, makes great the life. Try to be Shakespeare, leave the rest to fate."

James Keenan, S.J., *The Works of Mercy: The Heart of Catholicism* (Lanham, Maryland: Rowman & Littlefield Publisher, Inc., A Sheed & Ward Book, 2008), p. 4

In *Works of Mercy*, Father Keenan's theme is that God's mercy makes human love possible. This, Father Keenan says, he learned through relationships with family, friends, and his Jesuit community. Acts of mercy recall what God has done for us—for our own redemption and salvation. To show mercy—to show love—one must be willing to enter into the "chaos" of others.

Father Keenan has been a leader in bringing together Catholic theological ethicists from around the world. His goal: to encourage cross-cultural dialogue among ethicists and so to form connections within a world church, one that speaks mercifully to all peoples (including women) and is not dominated by traditional views. He has done so by organizing conferences that are nothing less than modern-day Councils of Trent in their aim to bring reform to the Catholic Church.

A Definition of Mercy
...the willingness to enter into the chaos of others.

—James Keenan, S.J.

I am struck by Father Keenan's use of the word "chaos." Our impulse may be to avoid entering into the problems of other people, but Keenan reminds us that an act of mercy, though it may expose us to chaos, also brings order to our own lives. In his work to bring together the diverse voices of the Catholic Church, Father Keenan has shown that he is willing to face "chaos" so that mercy may shine.

James Keenan, S.J., *The Works of Mercy:*
The Heart of Catholicism (Lanham, Maryland:
Rowman & Littlefield Publishers, Inc.,
A Sheed & Ward Book, 2008), pp. 133, 136

Father Keenan addresses mercy in our lives,
our family lives, and the world. He does
not shy from difficult subjects, such as the
Catholic Church's sexual abuse scandals.

Father Keenan writes very personally of entering into his own "chaos." In doing so, he
shares with the reader that his first step is to pray—"to ask God for the light, the
illumination, to see myself as I am, or better as God sees me."

We all know that entering into our own chaos is
a very disheveling event.
If I enter into another's at least, I can always
retrieve myself from my entrance.
I can tell the other person, I'll be back again, at another time.
I can steel myself for the next encounter.
Once I enter my own chaos, there's no turning back.
I am trapped in myself and by my own chaos
for I know I can't very well say to myself,
see you soon, I'll be back again.
Facing my own chaos is very daunting
Because inevitably I face it alone
I see what others can't see and I see what often I don't want to see.
And, then inevitably, I realize I need to do something about it…

Noteworthy, the first step is an act of prayer asking God
for the light, the illumination to see myself as I am,
or, better, as God sees me.
…As a Christian it is really only by God's grace and
with God's presence that I want to and can face my chaos.

—James Keenan, S.J.

Paul Tillich, *The Shaking of the Foundations: Sermons Applicable to the Personal and Social Problems of Religious Life* (New York: Charles Scribner's Sons, 1948), p. 161

Paul Tillich (1886–1965) was one of the most influential Protestant theologians and philosophers of the 20th century. The son of a conservative Prussian Lutheran minister, he brought Christian scripture to bear on philosophy's existential questions. Tillich's adult life spanned the horrors of the First World War, the decadence of Berlin in the 1920s, the rise of German Nazism, and emigration to the United States. In America, Tillich found a wide new audience, winning a reputation as a brilliant teacher and public intellectual. *The Shaking of the Foundations* is Tillich's first collection of sermons—an entry point for understanding his thinking on existential questions and insights provided by Christian revelation.

Grace strikes us when we are in great pain and restlessness...
Sometimes at that moment
a wave of light breaks into our darkness
and it is as though a voice were saying,
You are accepted. You are accepted..."

—Paul Tillich

My understanding of grace has shifted. I once saw the presence of grace when things were going well. Now, I also recognize moments of grace in breaks of light during the dark periods. The contrast between light and dark intensifies my appreciation for the gift of grace.

Sister Nancy Corcoran's voice-mail message at grass/roots, Women's Spirituality Center, an interfaith program that she founded.

Sister Corcoran, CSJ, is the director of the Newman Catholic Ministry at Wellesley College, and the author of *Secrets of Prayer: A Multifaith Guide to Creating Personal Prayer in Your Life.* The grass/roots program mission is "Create community, one conversation at a time."

Be a blessing for someone today.

—Sister Nancy Corcoran

When life brings us challenges,
we usually tell ourselves to be strong and others often do, too.
I think that the challenges are also an invitation
to acknowledge how much we need God's help.

Does being strong mean that we shouldn't ask for help? Maybe real strength is the ability to let go of the idea that we should be strong. Across time and often independently, many spiritual people have found that letting go, surrendering to God, becomes the source of their strength in the face of challenge. For the rest of us non-saints, such advice may be easier said than done, but asking for help can be a first step.

When pride comes, then comes disgrace,
with humility comes wisdom.

—Proverbs 11:2

Pride is a quality someone might observe in others, but not necessarily in himself or herself. When a person is disgraced, he or she becomes aware. But, how do we recognize true humility in ourselves?

The daughter, wife and mother of ministers, Catherine Marshall (1914–1983) was the author of a long list of bestselling inspirational books, both fiction and nonfiction. Her first book, *A Man Called Peter,* is a profile of her husband, Peter Marshall, who emigrated to the United States with few prospects, went to divinity school, began his ministry in a humble Southern parish, and rose to become the chaplain of the U.S. Senate. Written to preserve his memory and also for financial support, the book became a popular success and a major movie. It also launched Mrs. Marshall's writing career. Her *Christy* books, inspired by her mother's experience as a young teacher in Appalachia, were much loved as is her *Story Bible.* Her husband's sudden death and her own struggle with tuberculosis give Mrs. Marshall's books a depth that has contributed to their staying power.

When things get too much,
wrap them in a box and give them
to God to handle.

—Paraphrased from Catherine Marshall

I began reading Catherine Marshall's spiritual writings many years ago, and sometimes call on her image of a box for storing troubles when I am trying to carry too much on my own shoulders. Just the mental gesture or visualization can be a relief.

Welcoming pamphlet, the Society of Saint
John the Evangelist, Cambridge, Massachusetts

The Society of St. John the Evangelist
welcomes the public to its chapel in
Cambridge every day, except Monday, the
Brothers' Sabbath.

The arch image catches my imagination. Two weaknesses connected into a single strength. A joint redemption of weaknesses and the idea that a breakdown or breakup becomes a point of breakthrough for God. This thought helps me grasp that my goal shouldn't be perfection, but that my weaknesses, when joined, have the potential for making a strength.

We find the arch a strong and inspiring image.
The arch is also a paradoxical image [that] is built on weakness.
Many centuries ago Leonardo da Vinci wrote
that an arch is made up of two segments of a circle,
and each of these segments being in itself very weak desires to fall,
and as one withstands the downfall of the other,
the two weaknesses are converted into a single strength.
This redemption of weakness is also a reality
we brothers continually experience.
We know one another very well,
not just our strengths
but also our weaknesses.
A breakdown or breakup becomes
a point of breakthrough for God.
We so often witness God's strength being
perfected out of our weakness,
both in our life together as a community
and as we minister to others:
individuals confiding in us
their own experiences of suffering, grief and loss,
and their longing to know God's real presence
amidst God's seeming absence.

— Society of Saint John the Evangelist

There has been a lot of serendipity in my life.

While studying for my master's degree in career counseling,
I learned the career development theory of "happenstance."

Things happen to us when we have been getting ourselves ready,
even if we don't know for what.

"I just happened to sit next to this person on the bus and was given the name of someone to call about a job" or "I had a flat tire on the highway and the person who stopped to help me had a cousin who could find me a house." Write down some of these serendipitous instances or coincidences. We are more likely to remember when "synchronicity" occurs and not notice when things don't happen. I have experienced more than a few seemingly providential coincidences in my life. In researching other authors' passages for Living Lines, I have been struck by how many of these reflective souls have responded to chance occurrences, too.

Light some birthday candles and start making wishes.
Who said there was a limit to wish-making
or that wishes were limited to your birthday?

—My friend Jane

Don't put a period in a sentence
where there should be a comma.
God is still talking.

—Attributed to Gracie Allen

I saw this piece of advice—attributed to Gracie Allen—on a church sign years ago.
A beloved comedian of the 1950s, Gracie Allen was also a devout Catholic in a famously
happy marriage to George Burns, who was Jewish. (Burns's last role was God in
Oh, God! *and its sequels.) Allen's reflection—with its truth and humor—is one of my*
favorite lines.

Hope is a spiritual gift that begins with God,
God's hope in us.
It is not the same as optimism.
Optimism is a mere gloss.
Hope draws on the reservoir of your past.

If you are feeling hope-deprived, look backwards.
Draw from your memory what you already know about
sailing in uncharted waters.
How in the world have you faced what you've had to face
to get to be where you are? You are a walking miracle; you are
also an experienced navigator.
Recall St. Paul's formula, that "we boast in our sufferings, knowing that
suffering produces our endurance, and endurance produces character,
and character produces hope, and hope does not disappoint us, because
God's love has been poured into our hearts through the Holy Spirit that
has been given to us." Romans 5:1–5.
Hope is an anchor amidst the storms of life.

—*Hope Abiding,* Monastery Newsletter, Society of St. John the Evangelist, December 2008

Peace.
It does not mean to be in a place where
there is not noise, trouble, or hard work.
It means to be in the midst of those things
and still be calm in your heart.

—Unknown

Let go.
Let God.

Four simple words that are an invitation, a challenge, an opportunity. The exhortation to surrender to God runs from the ancient texts of the world's religions and meditation traditions to present-day interpretations. Not my will, but Yours.

St. Francis de Sales, as quoted in *A Selection from The Spiritual Letters of S. Francis de Sales* (London: Rivingtons, 1880) p. 161

St. Francis de Sales (1567–1622) was an evangelical preacher and writer, who became Catholic Bishop of Geneva. Born the eldest son of aristocratic French parents, Francis de Sales was intended to follow a secular, magisterial life with a well-born wife. Parental expectations did not come to pass. A long crisis of despair as a teenager lifted after de Sales saw a miraculous vision of the Virgin Mary. The young saint-to-be then committed himself to a life of simplicity and chastity, dedicated to God. His inner turmoil over predestination (the theological issue of his age) gave way to an acceptance of whatever God had in store for him. De Sales believed in the scriptural God of Love, and his writings and sermons gave spiritual direction founded in a confidence in God. His *Introduction to the Devout Life* is a spiritual classic, read by both Catholics and Protestants. Known and loved for his goodness, patience, and pleasant nature, Francis de Sales was canonized less than 50 years after his death.

Father George Salzmann, who is a chaplain at Harvard and a member of the order founded by St. Francis de Sales, often quotes his order's patron saint, "Do everything through love and nothing through fear."

Do not look forward to the changes and chances of this life in fear;
rather look forward to them with full hope,
that as they arise, God, whose you are,
will deliver you safely out of them.
He has kept you hitherto—do you but hold fast to His dear hand,
and He will lead you safely through all things;
and when you cannot stand,
He will bear you in His arms...
Do not look forward to what may happen tomorrow;
the same everlasting Father who cares for you today
will take care of you tomorrow, and every day.
Either He will shield you from suffering
or He will give you unfailing strength to bear it.
Be at peace then,
and put aside all anxious thoughts and imaginations...

—St. Francis de Sales

Zen Buddhists say, "Chop wood; carry water." Just do the next thing in your path, and your path will become clearer.

Zen Buddhism is a distinct school of Buddhism that emerged in China around 700 C.E. In Zen, the focus is less on theoretical knowledge than on experiential realization gained through meditation and virtue.

"What do you do before Enlightenment?" Buddha was asked.
"Chop wood;
Carry water."
"What do you do after enlightenment?"
"Chop wood;
Carry water."

Routine tasks are reassuring. Unless you have a rustic cabin in the deep in the woods, you won't need to chop wood or carry water, but there are still plenty of routine daily tasks in modern life—unloading the dishwasher, folding laundry, filing papers, sponging kitchen countertops, to name a few. If I approach such work with discipline, the extra effort seems to make the day brighter, giving a satisfaction that strengthens body, mind, and spirit.

Thomas Carlyle, "Labor," *Past and Present* (1843)

Thomas Carlyle (1795–1881)—eminent Victorian essayist and historian—was another producer of aphorisms, still very much in circulation today. (It was Carlyle who famously called economics "the dismal science.") Born in a small Scottish village to strict Calvinist parents, Carlyle was expected to become a preacher. However, as a young man he suffered a crisis of belief and lost his faith in traditional Christianity. Instead of the Kirk, he pursued the not unrelated path of a social observer and critic, perhaps a more fitting role given his satirical gifts. Nevertheless, Carlyle's spiritual nature showed through in his writing. Carlyle formed a lifelong friendship with the slightly younger Ralph Waldo Emerson, who served as Carlyle's unofficial literary agent in the United States. A measure of Emerson's success in representing Carlyle may be that quotation dictionaries devote impressively lengthy space to his Scottish friend.

Blessed is he who has found his work;
let him ask no other blessedness.

—Thomas Carlyle

Most people must work to earn a living; someone who works with a passion is blessed. However, if one's work isn't a passion, Carlyle offers this, "Every day that is born into the world comes like a burst of music and rings the whole day through, and you make of it a dance, a dirge, or a life march, as you will."

Brother David Steindl-Rast, *A Listening Heart: The Spirituality of Sacred Sensuousness* (New York: Crossroad Publishing Company, 1999), p. 116

Brother David Steindal-Rast (1926–) is a philosopher and Benedictine monk. Born in Austria, he emigrated to the United States as a young man, and so had the opportunity to see the world around him with fresh, grateful eyes. In the 1960s, he received the Vatican's permission to study Buddhism, thus refreshing his perceptions of the world once again. For four decades, Brother David has divided his time between periods of a hermit's life and extensive lecture tours on five continents. He is a leading figure in the movement to renew religious life and form prayer communities.

Living Lines

Gratitude is a passage
from suspicion to trust
from isolation to give and take,
from independence to interdependence.

—Brother David Steindl-Rast

Ten years ago, I was invited to dinner at a neighbor's home. Sitting next to me on the sofa was a Benedictine monk, who—to my surprise—told me he was a hermit. It was Brother David Steindl-Rast, a hermit with a Website, who has written seven books and many articles on spirituality and Buddhist-Christian dialogue.

Brother David Steindl-Rast, *A Listening Heart: The Spirituality of Sacred Sensuousness* (New York: Crossroad Publishing Company, 1999) p. 56

The doxology cited by Brother Steindl-Rast was written by English clergyman, Thomas Ken (1637–1711) in the 1670s. Ken's familiar line is the first of the final stanza of morning and evening hymns. Written for the devotions of students at Winchester College, Ken instructed that they be recited privately in chambers. At the time, Church of England establishment believed that only lines of Scripture were appropriate for hymns. To write new hymns was considered by some to be blasphemous.

Thomas Ken lived during one of England's most tumultuous centuries. Educated at Oxford, Ken consecrated himself to God as a young man. He was a skilled musician, and loved holy music, which was silenced under the rule of Oliver Cromwell. With restoration of the monarchy, church music began to sound again, and Ken became a spiritual adviser to King Charles II. Though he famously refused to let Charles's mistress, Nell Gwyn, stay at his Winchester lodgings, he was nonetheless the king's favorite prelate and the king later named him a bishop. During the reign of James II, Ken resisted the restoration of "popery," and was tried for treason. He was acquitted, but lost his bishopric upon the ascension of William III. He accepted poverty gracefully and was said to love to be alone with his God. The historian Lord Macaulay described Ken as having a moral character that seemed "to approach, as near as any human infirmity permits, to the ideal of Christian perfection." Ken's great Morning Hymn was sung at his funeral, held fittingly at sunrise.

Praise God, from Whom all blessings flow:
Praise Him, all creatures here below;
Praise Him above, ye angelic host,
Praise Father, Son and Holy Ghost.

Blessing is the spiritual lifeblood throbbing through the universe.
"Praise God from Whom all blessings flow."

—Brother David Steindl-Rast

I love the thought of blessings coursing through the universe, particularly the beautiful line of praise from Thomas Ken's 17th-century hymn. Much loved and widely translated, Ken's hymn is sung in churches of all Christian denominations throughout the liturgical year. On Sundays especially, it is easy to imagine the words and melody—"Praise God from Whom all blessings flow"—encircling the earth.

Brother David Steindl-Rast, *Gratefulness,*
The Heart of Prayer: An Approach to Life in
Fullness (New Jersey: Paulist Press, 1984),
p. 10, 12

Surprise is…a beginning of the fullness we call gratefulness.
…What counts on your path to fulfillment is that
we remember the great truth that moments of surprise
want to teach us:
…everything is [a] gift.
The degree to which we are awake to this truth is the
measure of our gratefulness.
And gratefulness is the measure of our aliveness.

—Brother David Steindl-Rast

For Brother David Steindl-Rast, the sudden appearance of a rainbow captures the essence of surprise and the awakening of gratefulness. He notes that even an adult, who has seen it all before, finds excitement in a rainbow. And who, he asks, doesn't find the renewal of spring—the emergence of gorgeous blossoms and singing birds—a surprise? Moments of surprise are gifts. And the more alive we are to these gifts, the fuller our hearts and lives. Long before I ever read Brother Steindl-Rast's books, I intuitively looked for surprises in the world around me. His core symbol of surprise is the rainbow; mine is the butterfly…

Spirituality

The message of Brother Steindl-Rast is
elegantly summarized by Henri J.M. Nouwen,
in the forward to Brother Steindl-Rast,
Gratefulness: The Heart of Prayer (New Jersey:
Paulist Press, 1984), p. 4

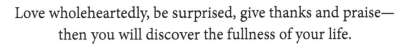

Love wholeheartedly, be surprised, give thanks and praise—
then you will discover the fullness of your life.

— Brother Steindl-Rast

Mary Oliver, *Thirst* (Boston: Beacon Press Books, 2006), p. 1

Mary Oliver has published 15 volumes of poetry since her first at the age of 28. Not a writer to seek publicity, Ms. Oliver is nevertheless a best-selling poet. She published "Messenger" in the year following the death of her partner of more than 40 years.

Mary Oliver's elegant poems direct the reader to survey the simple things of the natural world, and in doing so, to find gratitude. It seems fitting to give her poem "Messenger" one of the final pages of these Living Lines, so that her words may ring in your heart as they do in mine.

Messenger

My work is loving the world.
Here the sunflowers, there the hummingbird—
    equal seekers of sweetness.
Here the quickening yeast; there the blue plums.
Here the clam deep in the speckled sand.

Are my boots old? Is my coat torn?
Am I no longer young, and still not half-perfect? Let me
    keep my mind on what matters,
which is my work,

which is mostly standing still and learning to be
    astonished.
The phoebe, the delphinium.
The sheep in the pasture, and the pasture.
Which is mostly rejoicing, since all ingredients are here,

which is gratitude, to be given a mind and a heart
    and these body-clothes,
a mouth with which to give shouts of joy
    to the moth and the wren, to the sleepy dug-up clam,
telling them all, over and over, how it is
    that we live forever.

—Mary Oliver

Finally, I ask you the questions that I hold in my heart:

How are you?
Who are you?
Are you living in fullness?

Afterword

When I was growing up in a large suburb of New York, the community, including my neighborhood, was full of families—Catholic, Protestant of all denominations, and Jewish. Though the children played together, we weren't quite a melting pot. As a Catholic, I absorbed certain expectations: Catholic children went to Catholic schools; Catholics girls dated (and married) Catholic boys; Catholics received medical care at Catholic hospitals, and were buried in Catholic cemeteries. I remember being puzzled that I was not allowed to go to my Protestant friends' churches or my Jewish friends' synagogues for services, including weddings and funerals. Nor were my friends of other religions permitted to go to my church. Somehow, caroling on Christmas Eve was an exception, and my friends—Catholic, Protestant and Jewish—enjoyed this once-a-year sharing.

By the time I was in high school, some of the barriers were quietly falling away—even in my own family. My parents sent my brother—ten years younger than I—to public school! When a priest from a neighboring all-boys' school came to my all girls' school during my senior year to teach a marriage course, he predicted that probably over half of us would marry a non-Catholic. "Oh, no, Father, how could that be!" Well, that was 1960, and just over four years later, I married an Episcopalian, and the same priest married us.

These pages reflect my personal journey and continuing spiritual search. What I have shared here is not intended to be a comprehensive road map to different faiths, but to offer reflections that I have found meaningful. Though I remain a Christian, it is obvious that Jewish wisdom speaks to my heart. As for the Buddhist tradition, it has expanded my understanding of human psychology, and thanks to His Holiness the Dalai Lama, it has introduced me to neuroscience, a field that has so much potential for contributing to human wellbeing.

In my autobiographical introduction, I shared many of the events of my life that have shaped me as a religious and spiritual person. Like other people, I am a product of my times. During my adult life, the background conversation about religion in the United States has been constant and loud, even shrill. When I was in college, it was Friedrich Nietzsche's "God is dead" challenge to religion, proclaimed on sweatshirts and echoed on a famous "Is God Dead?" *Time* magazine cover in 1966. As if on cue, priests and nuns and Ivy League college chaplains stepped forward as leaders of the protests against the Vietnam War. Then, in another powerful wave, evangelical Christians asserted themselves as a political force, even as the Palestinian-Israeli conflict established itself as regular front-page news. And since the 1970s, Americans have become increasingly aware of Islam.

For the most part, Americans have responded to this religious ferment with tolerance and renewed interest in religion. Recent titles like, *The Twilight of Atheism* and *God Is Back,* suggest that belief in God continues. (Of course, opposing titles—*God Is Not Great*—sell well, too.) And the interest in religion is not without humor. For example, religion contributes to the story line of almost every episode of *The Simpsons.* Or consider a "Nietzsche Is Dead" T-shirt; the intent is to draw a laugh, not to shock.

Pollsters tell us that Americans see themselves as a religious people. Even so, more and more people are seeking spiritual paths that are separate from established religions. Thanks to the religious faith of my parents, my quest to understand the meaning of life started early. And thanks to the times, I've been able to explore across traditions, looking beyond the Catholicism in which I was baptized. When I was a young woman, my interest in religion wasn't so widely shared. Sometimes now, with the current outpouring of interest, there is more and more to explore and consider. Though my search continues, I have created this book as a gift for my family, friends, and others who might discover Living Lines and find inspiration for their own journeys.

Afterword

Acknowledgments